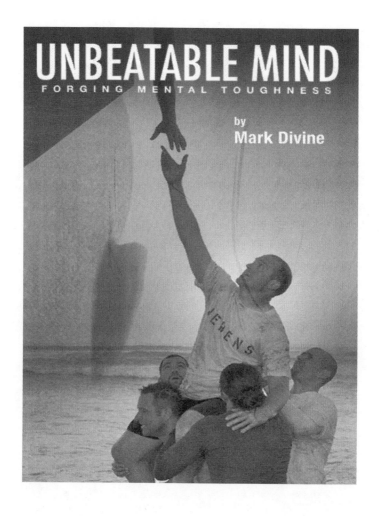

UNBEATABLE MIND
FORGING MENTAL TOUGHNESS

by
Mark Divine

UNBEATABLE
MIND

Forge Resiliency and Mental Toughness
to Succeed at an Elite Level

MARK DIVINE

UNBEATABLE
MIND

MARK DIVINE

Dedicated to my son, Devon

CONTENTS

Introduction: This Is Unbeatable Mind   1
A Foundation of Silence   3
Teams 'n' Shit   6
Part-Time SEAL, Full-Time Entrepreneur   10
Yoga Jitsu   12
The Unbeatable Mind Road Map   13

Section 1: Uncover Your Why and Positively Focus It

Chapter One: Win in the Mind   21
"Seeing" the Win   25
Embracing Sacred Silence   26
The Witness   27
Starving Fear, Feeding Courage   28
Exercise 1: The Fishbowl Visualization   32

Chapter Two: Training the Brain Zoo   35
The Brain Zoo   36
Shortcut the Gladwell Effect   45
Exercise 2: Intro to Journaling   47

Chapter Three: Emotional Resiliency   48
The 3Ps and Your One Thing   49
Emotional Resiliency   50
The Big Four of Emotional Resiliency   55
Exercise 3: Defining Your 3Ps and Your One Thing   57

Chapter Four: Mental Toughness   60
Understanding and Managing Stress   64
Double-Barrel Power: Breathing and Concentration   67
Concentration through Breathwork   69

Breath Control Basic Training   72
Box Breathing   75
Exercise 4: Box Breathing with Positive Fuel   77

Section 2: Cultivate Excellence

Chapter Five: Self-Mastery   79
The Five Mountains   81
The Six Disciplines of the Warrior   85
Simplicity   85
Dedication   87
Authenticity   89
"MURPH"   90
Compassion   91
Abundance   92
Generosity   93
Writing Your Own Script   95
Exercise 5: Write Your Own Script   96

Chapter Six: Deep Awareness   100
Three-Sphere Awareness   101
Your Background of Obviousness   109
Aligning with Universal Laws   113
Exercise 6: Insight Meditation   120

Chapter Seven: Trust and Humility   124
Trustworthiness   126
Leadership   130
Humility   134
Responsibility   136
Determination   139
Perseverance   139
The Navy SEAL Ethos   142
Exercise 7: Contemplation   144

Chapter Eight: Fail Forward Fast   146
KISS Planning   147
SMARTP-FITS Goals   148
F3 and OODA Loop   153
Visualize Success   156
Exercise 8: Create a SMARTP-FITS Goal   159

Section 3: The Integrated Self in Action

Chapter Nine: Sheepdog Strong   162
The Sheep and the Wolves   163
Here Are Some Rules of Engagement   165
Offensive Mindset   167
Dog Training   168
Exercise 9: The Body Scan   172

Chapter Ten: The Integrated Self   176
The Five Plateaus   179
Wake Up, Grow Up, and Clean Up to Show Up   182
First Plateau: The Survivor   184
Second Plateau: The Protector   186
Third Plateau: The Achiever   187
Fourth Plateau: The Equalizer   189
Fifth Plateau: The Integrator   191
Leading from the Fifth Plateau   192
Exercise 10: Identify Your Plateau and Set a Goal   195

Afterword
Ten Secrets to Success
About the Author
Staring Down the Wolf
Kokoro Yoga
Resources

The Body Is the Feeler of Emotions and Sensations

The Mind Is the Thinker of Thoughts

The Witness Is the Observer of All

— Sensei Shane Phelps

UNBEATABLE
MIND

THIS IS UNBEATABLE MIND

"When a man is beaten, tormented and defeated...He is ready to learn something."

— Emerson

Over the years I see the same remarkable situation and state of being, again and again, in the thousands who have joined my SEALFIT and Unbeatable Mind Programs. These individuals are exceptionally accomplished by society's standards, with fine careers and ample success to report in their professional and personal lives. But from my discussions with the new trainees, it's long become apparent to me that regardless of their success, they feel stuck in a low gear. They feel incomplete, half-empty, conscious that they could be giving far more, but unable to break out of an ingrained pattern of mediocrity.

For some in the world, an existential threat, like a fight with cancer, will shatter their complacency and free them from such a rut onto a higher level of thought and action. But my trainees don't wait for an accident of fate to spur their change. They seek to take charge and drill down into their full potential so that they have the power to make a difference in the world.

I bet you feel the same way. The good news is that you now have a tool in your hands that will guide you forward in solving this frustrating puzzle of the human experience. The "big idea" of this book is that you are capable of far more than you think you are — more accomplishment, more productivity, more success — but you have been kept in the dark about this potential your entire life. I call this potential your **20X Factor**, in that you are capable of accelerating you daily achievement by twenty times what your current paradigm allows you to believe is possible. It is not as though your family, or our culture, purposely kept you in the dark about this important fact. Rather, they were ignorant about it as well and can't be held to blame. We cannot ignore this truth any longer. Not only do you deserve to unleash your full potential for your own success and happiness, society needs your optimal output to confront the grave problems that mire modern civilization. These problems are of such a complex and deep-rooted nature I believe our collective minds are needed to sync up like a global crowd-sourced network of solution finders to pull us out of the mess we have created. This book isn't an exploration of the various messes, though — there are plenty of authors reporting about the perils we face on our abused planet. This book is about how you can begin to open a channel to that vast potential lying dormant inside of you — so that you can achieve your fullest expression of yourself, help those around you, and send positive ripples throughout the world.

A Foundation of Silence

Let me back up now and give you an idea of where I'm coming from and how I got here.

In my early childhood, I learned to find solace in the peace and silence of nature. And growing up in the mountains and valleys of the Adirondacks in Upstate New York (Upstate, as we call it, covers 95 percent of the real estate of New York—the other 5 percent is squeezed into the New York Metro area.), all I had to do was step out the back door to find it. My father's love for the trails, combined with my mother's athleticism, kept us outdoors. Twice a week during the summer I would find myself navigating the Adirondack peaks with my dad and Brad, my brother. I cherished these expeditions. They struck me with a sense of awe for the natural beauty and excitement of always finding something new around the next bend in the trail.

I became comfortable with the silence. I had no idea at the time, but this would prove to become a bedrock theme in my life. Nature never argued with me and, as long as I respected her, made no significant demands. Often, I would just sit in absorption, not thinking or striving for anything in particular, and allow the peace to settle in.

On the home front, things were loud and often confusing as my parents fought routinely. For reasons I did not understand at the time, I was shut down and unsettled, locked in a prison constructed of my own conflicting emotions. I craved the contentment and connection that I felt so keenly when alone in nature, but I had no luck finding it in relationships. So my relationship with nature was a friendship I would turn to often, through solitude

3

and silence tuning into that awesome power, and I can tell you now that this was the mentor relationship that prepared me most for what was to be my future as a warrior.

In high school, I made lettering in sports a pastime that carried into my college years as well. Though I enjoyed the camaraderie of team sports, I was drawn to the simplicity and psychological challenge of endurance athletics. Endless laps in the pool and running track were predominantly mental endeavors. Through these sports I learned the importance of proper breathing and the basics of managing the mind. My high school swim times earned me a slot on the Colgate University team, and off I went in 1981.

I settled on a major in economics, thinking that it would help when I landed back at Divine Brothers, Inc., a legacy family business in manufacturing started in 1898. Socially, my world burst wide open as I began a love affair with beer and women (prioritized in that order, it's fair to mention). After a semester of unhinged craziness, I knew I needed to settle down and anchor myself or I would drift off even further, or altogether drown, so I recommitted to the drill I knew best: nature and sports. The rigor of my daily schedule kept me focused and less prone to participate in the nonstop party.

I'd be lying if I didn't admit those were great times, and I have some great friends from that era. However, I was clueless as to what I wanted to do when I grew up beside the family business, which was my default plan. And as to the measure of when I was grown up, I was running out of room even by the most liberal of definitions. As senior year ground to a close, though, I found myself with a unique job offer from a Big 8 CPA firm in Manhattan. The firm Coopers & Lybrand (now PricewaterhouseCoopers) somehow figured it a sound investment to sponsor me to attend the NYU Stern School of Business as part of a work-study program. I would work as an auditor for two years, during which time I would get a master's and pass the CPA exam.

So, within five weeks of graduating Colgate, I found myself back in summer school at NYU. For a few months, the newness of the challenge motivated me, but it wasn't long before I dreaded the monotony of the "real world." Was this really what I was going to do for the rest of my life? Completely on my own now, I was overwrought as the educational bills piled up and my options for escape dwindled. I started to openly question whether I had made a disastrous mistake from which there was no turning back.

Walking home from the subway one Manhattan evening, I was snapped out of these sorts of dire thoughts when I heard spirited shouts exploding from a second-floor window. Looking up, I noted a flag stating "SEIDO Karate, World Headquarters." Interesting. Sounds like they are whipping up a storm up there, I thought. I couldn't resist, so I climbed the stairs and met the man who would become my first mentor, who held the key to unlock the door to my own Unbeatable Mind.

Kaicho (Grandmaster) Tadashi Nakamura founded Seido Karate in the seventies. He was brought to the United States by Mas Oyama, the founder of Kyokushinkai Karate to head up the tradition's training in this country as it was gaining in popularity and spreading quickly. After a few years, Nakamura became disenchanted with the tournament fighting focus of that style, desiring to teach karate in combination with Zen training to a broader base of students. He believed that the inner development of the warrior must parallel the outer development, or the art could be used improperly. In essence he felt that self-mastery was equally as important as fighting prowess. The fighting strategies, tactics, techniques, and physical conditioning were methods of the outer training, while meditation, contemplation, and silence were the methods of inner warrior development. Incidentally, most modern martial arts have lost this subtle art of warrior development, aiming instead at competition or MMA-style training. Kaicho Nakamura's training and mentorship caused a paradigm shift in my own consciousness — meeting him was a watershed moment in my life. My experience of life after Seido was, well, different.

I received my Shodan black belt ranking in November of 1989. I also received my CPA and my MBA certificates the same month. But the most significant thing that happened that November was that I hopped on a train to Newport, Rhode Island, to begin my second career as a naval officer. The mentorship I had received under Kaicho Nakamura's guidance had opened my vision to new avenues of possibility, and I charged ahead on one of the more adventurous ones — I had become enchanted with the Navy SEALs' siren call to "Be Someone Special." In short, I took the bait. Into the Navy I went in 1989 and never looked back.

Teams 'n' Shit

It was late November when I disembarked in Newport, Rhode Island, leaving behind the suit, the corporate world, and sadly, Kaicho Nakamura. Officer Candidate School (OCS) was four months of marching from one class to another in formation, and I gutted through it, no problem. It's an understatement to say that things would heat up. In March, now in Coronado, California, I checked into BUD/S, the six-month SEAL training course for Class 171. It was a Friday, and I was informed my class wouldn't begin for another ten weeks and that a different class, 170, was ramping up that coming Monday. I was determined to get started right away, so I went searching for someone who could make it happen.

My determined search had me stepping onto the deck of the Combat Training Tank (SEAL-speak for swimming pool) facing the 180 panic-stricken looking students of class 170, lorded over by Lieutenant Rick May perched high on the dive platform. The entire class went silent when this newly minted officer (me) entered their space.

"What can we do for you, Enzyme?" was May's response to my interruption.

"Sir, I have orders to 171 but would like to class up with 170," I said with a sense of confidence.

"OK, that's not normal. Prove to us that you are ready: swim fifty meters underwater in your boots and Utes (utility pants) right now," he said.

OK, I thought, this is going to be interesting, but it's right up my alley.

The sea of candidates parted, likely evaluating my sanity during this brazen stunt. I stood at the pool's edge, took a few deep breaths, and jumped in, boots and all. I pulled like hell against the water and made it to the other side, and then I turned and kicked against the wall with all my might. I glided halfway and then pulled my way to the

other side. Gassed, I could barely drag myself onto the deck
to await sentencing.

"See me Monday morning," May said. Then he went
back to hammering the class.

On Monday, I classed up with 170. May and the other
SEAL instructors were a different breed of men than I had
ever been exposed to. Their confidence was born not of
cockiness, the view from their skyscraper office, or the size
of their paycheck, but of extreme competence and a "been
there, done that" air of untouchability. Legend had it that
Lieutenant May fractured his leg on the third day of his
Hell Week. He wasn't going to let an annoying little detail
like that sideline him, so he continued to run on it until he
passed out from the pain...after securing from training on
day five!

People like Lieutenant May and Lieutenant Zinke were
my heroes and new mentors for the next nine months. They
never messed around, or wasted time, preferring to go
from zero to a hundred miles per hour on day one and not
throttling back at all for the duration. The training
standards kept getting harder and faster while the quitting
line got longer. Those of us who had spent several years
preparing and cultivating our mental toughness were
ready. Those who had not, were not—and didn't survive.
Of the 180 who started in my SEAL training class, only
nineteen graduated. I was the Honor Man of the class.

The arduous BUD/S training has been exposed by
many SEAL authors and Hollywood movies, so I won't
review the details here. But I will sprinkle in a few
anecdotal stories to back up a principle here and there.
Before I go on, for you ladies reading this, I want you to
know that this book is every bit as much for you as it is for

the guys. Though the SEALs and martial arts are dominated by rough-and-tumble men, I have trained alongside many women in the arts and, more recently, in the discipline of Ashtanga Yoga. In Ashtanga most of my peers are women, every one of them as physically capable, or more so, than their male counterparts. The principles of Unbeatable Mind are not about being hard-core but rather about how to perform at your peak in any domain, whether you are a mom, dad, SEAL, student, or CPA.

After BUD/S training, I was ordered to join SEAL Team 3 in Coronado. There I was assigned as assistant platoon commander of Alpha Platoon under Lieutenant Washabau.

Wash was an excellent officer, and we trained the team hard for twelve months. We were slated to go to Desert Storm. We were just heading out the door when the war ended, so instead we deployed to the Philippines. In the "PI" we conducted a mission confusingly called "Foreign Internal Defense" (FID was a term used to describe US Special Operations Forces training a foreign force for their internal defense needs) and other special reconnaissance missions. FID had us train a number of naval special ops forces in the Asian rim for the purpose of bilateral relations, point of presence, cultural awareness, and intelligence.

I really enjoyed these missions, though they paled in comparison to the hard-core direct-action missions seen by the SEALs since 9/11. Most of all I loved working with Alpha Platoon and SEAL Team 3, serving there for close to five years. The work was fast paced, extremely challenging, and rewarding. Some of the stories that came out of that period are outrageously funny and mind-blowing. We chalked all those experiences up to what we called "teams 'n' shit." Most SEALs who stick around for more than a single tour have a set of crazy sea stories to tell due to the nature of the team and the missions taken on.

In 1995, my Platoon Commander Tour ST-3 was cut short, and I was assigned to SEAL Delivery Vehicle Team 1 in Hawaii. I also got married to a Coronado girl named Sandy. Learning how to drive and navigate the minisubs was almost as fun as learning how to navigate a marriage! When I checked into the team instead of going into another operating platoon, I was slotted to head up a special project that took me back to South Korea.

At this point in my active-duty SEAL career, I felt pulled in opposite directions. My wife was not thrilled about the massive amount of travel, and I did not want to be away from her for eleven months out of the year. I certainly understood the travel needs when I got married, but I wasn't prepared for the emotional challenge they presented. Many people dealt with this by treating their marriage like a business arrangement — it didn't bother them, and they enjoyed being away. I, on the other hand, didn't like it one bit. I worried that the marriage wouldn't survive the stress of constant deployment. In retrospect, I think that because I had such a difficult time connecting when I was younger, when I finally found a heart connection with a woman, I didn't want to blow it. Therefore, I made the difficult and life-changing decision to leave active duty and transfer to the SEAL Reserves.

Part-Time SEAL, Full-Time Entrepreneur

The Reserves left me with more free time than I'd had in my life since college, so I started to divert my energy to something new. In April of 1996, I paired up with my brother-in-law to launch the Coronado Brewing Company (CBC). It was only the third brewery to open in San Diego early in the trend, and the business is thriving to this day. Since that fateful decision I have launched five more successful businesses, including NavySEALs.com, Inasoft, US Tactical, US CrossFit, and SEALFIT. While busy as an entrepreneur, I also served at Reserve SEAL Teams 1, 3, and 17, as well as Naval Special Warfare Group ONE and Special Operations Command Pacific. I was mobilized for one-year active-duty stints twice, one time to Bahrain and Africa and the other to Iraq. There, I ran a special project with ST-1 to study whether the Marine Corps should become part of the special ops' community. I was also hired as an adjunct professor of leadership at the University of San Diego and helped launch an entrepreneurial leadership institute there. I was very busy, but again I felt like something was missing, just as I had back in my pre-SEAL days.

I thought back through the years and it was plain to me I was happiest and most successful when I was actively engaged in daily comprehensive training. With such a heavy focus on business for the last several years of my life, I'd shifted away from the integral training approach that had given me so much. Sure, I'd work out three to four times a week, but not as intensely or holistically as I had when training with Seido Karate or the SEALs. Also, I didn't have a team to train with, which makes a big difference in accountability. My life had become all work, and more importantly, just about getting things done. There was scant attention paid to physical training or mental performance, and no focus on growth and development. For a second time I was faced with the prospect of a slide into physical and mental mediocrity, and I decided I would find a way, or make a way, to train like I had in the Teams and at Seido ten years earlier.

Yoga Jitsu

In 1999, I essentially stumbled upon Saito Ninjitsu and Ashtanga Yoga and took them both up. Through my Ninjitsu training, I was able to tap into the physicality and raw warrior spirit of the martial arts again. It was liberating. But it was through the eight limbs of Ashtanga Yoga that I finally understood what it took to move from being a warrior athlete and leader to becoming a metaphorical warrior monk. Yoga turned me inside out, slowed me down and firmly planted a meditative practice back into my life. It was the perfect complement to the hard physical training that I was so accustomed to.

Yoga reinforced the notion that daily training and practice was more important than any specific teacher or skill. The journey of disciplining and "yoking" (the word Yoga means to yoke) the body, mind, and spirit to still itself and focus on higher-order notions of being and living is one of the great secrets to personal development. Just as the body will atrophy without constant training, the mind and spirit will not develop, and will atrophy, without a similar focus.

I began to experiment by combining CrossFit, Ninjitsu and Ashtanga techniques into my training regimen. I found each to be rich and rewarding, but alone they did not meet my warrior development goals. CrossFit lacked the inner development, Ninjitsu lacked the functional fitness and meditation, and yoga lacked the strength, stamina, work capacity, and endurance training I desired. So, I cobbled together a program with all three, but I found it difficult to handle three $150 monthly training memberships and juggle the schedules. So in 2006 I finally decided I would figure out a way to integrate the best of each system into one training model. The result, launched in 2007, was SEALFIT.

The training worked very well. In fact, it was so fun, effective, and uplifting that, by 2014, SEALFIT was known worldwide for our warrior development training. Along the way I had become a recognized mental toughness expert. All of this came from my desire to share with others the powerful training program I originally designed for myself that integrated the most powerful elements of physical, mental, emotional, intuitional, and spiritual training I could find.

The Unbeatable Mind Road Map

Since leaving the active-duty SEALs in 1996, I have watched how business and life have become so much faster, more complex, and more aggressive. The rules that I knew then have been shattered by the Internet and the diffusion of technology — forces that have seemed to flatten the world and increased the velocity of time. Entire cultures that were once isolated are now connected via mobile devices, and values are experiencing unprecedented rates of collision with differing viewpoints and ideas. The business landscape now has the look and feel of enemy territory on a clandestine SEAL mission. You and I must develop fresh, innovative methods and beliefs to effectively deal with this stark new reality.

Einstein said that you can't solve a problem from within the same paradigm the problem originated. In *Unbeatable Mind*, I offer a new model of personal enrichment that will enable your elevation to what I call the "Fifth Plateau" of consciousness. This is achieved by training and integrating five key lines of human development, which I call the "five mountains." They are your physical, emotional, mental, intuitional, and spiritual intelligences. This paradigm includes learning how to avoid damaging psychological loops and traps, developing new patterns of thinking that are positive and supercharged, and working from the "we" perspective rather than your narrow "I" perspective. When we can accomplish these things together, even on a small scale, not only will we forge our individual body-mind-spirits, but we will protect and better our children's future. Ultimately Unbeatable Mind is about developing your personal power fully so you can be more successful in your job, career, and life and then use your growing power to help guide your tribes, organizations, and the human race to a better place. Self-mastery, then service. Sounds lofty, right? If you are on board with this vision, then let's get busy learning how to forge your Unbeatable Mind!

Section 1: Uncover Your Why and Positively Focus It
Remember when you took that class to learn how to think about your thinking? What about that other class, where you were taught visualization to create optimal conditions for future success? What about the one on breathwork to

destress and tap into your intuition? Wait, what? Those classes weren't offered in your school? Well, they weren't offered in mine either. I am still waiting for these simple, profoundly beneficial tools to be taught to our youth, and I intend to ensure that happens. Face it; if you're not training your mind deliberately with proven tools and methods, then your identity, beliefs, and conditioning are being trained by family, peers, and your environment.

In Section 1, we're going to close the gap by learning how to win over a mind that has been trained poorly by our culture at large. An untrained and undisciplined mind will obsess, bounce from one distraction to another, and wreak havoc on motivation with relentless negative input, depleting you of your life force and creative energy. The Buddhists called this chaos the *monkey mind*. They are not referring to the mind of a cute and cuddly monkey, the kind you'd want as a pet — but the nastiest of enemies. The untrained mind is not your friend. It is your ego throwing shit at you, stealing your hopes and dreams, and locking you in the house of commons. The trained and disciplined mind, on the other hand, is a calm and steady ally, always positive and infinitely creative, ready to lead when called upon or follow your spirit's guidance without question or doubt. I'll show you how to achieve focus, determine where to target your efforts, and how to maintain that focus positively.

Once we learn how to find and focus this aspect of our minds, we will then begin the process of examining the quality of mental content, especially the negative thought streams and fear loops. It's imperative that you're able to control your mental focus so you can shift away from those influences.

Section 2: Cultivate Excellence

Forging an unbeatable mind requires virtuosity, not only our training but for every task we take on, from the mundane to the crucial. Consider that "the way you do anything is the way you do everything." This motivator will get you to pay close and mindful attention to every task – from laundry to playing with your child to studying for the Bar. In Section 2, I'll introduce you to box breathing, meditation, visualization techniques, and journaling – training tools that will allow you to cultivate excellence and attention to details. These and other *Unbeatable Mind* techniques will become daily companions, helping you to cultivate a deep self-awareness. You will begin to see the conditioned biases that plague your thinking and decision making. And these tools will help you to replace old conditioning with beliefs and behaviors grounded in universal truths. Cultivating excellence with these methods will become a daily cornerstone on your path to self-mastery. And, with time, these new skills will become breath-and-blood habits.

You will need to challenge yourself to slow down enough every day and use the tools, however. This is how you will "win in your mind before stepping onto the battle." This is how we do things a little bit differently than everyone else and become a little bit more unique and special.

Day by day, in every way, stronger and better, hooyah-hey!

Section 3: The Integrated Self in Action

In the third and final section, we will bring all our new skills, tools, and disciplines to the task of defining our missions and crushing our worthy goals.

In the SEALs, the trident is a gold emblem awarded at the completion of the arduous year-long training program — only the very best earn their place as a legendary SEAL. It symbolizes an enormous rite of passage into a special brotherhood bearing a strong sense of duty, professionalism, and service. However, that trident can be liberated from a SEAL if their ego convinces them they've "made it." Trust me when I say, "There is no there, there!" What is there is the constant effort to grow and improve every single day. That is what we mean by "earning your trident every day." It is the same with forging an unbeatable mind.

You've had some major breakthroughs? Great, now move on.

You're finding flow routinely? Good job, now move on. What's next?

The point is to show up as the highest and best version of yourself, in service, day in and day out. That is how we unlock accelerating development and become whole. That is how we tame the ego and live from spiritual principles. Just as a SEAL quickly learns that his actions determine whether he gets to keep his trident and the trust of his teammates, so will you earn your trident and trust anew each and every day.

The only easy day was yesterday because it is gone. It's over. Tomorrow is hopefully going to come but there are no absolute guarantees there. So, guess what? It's all about

17

today. This is where you need to target your positive thoughts and creative energy. Today, there's respect to earn, training to accomplish, and meaningful success to work toward. You've got to show up and put in 100 percent to prove to your family and teams that you can be relied on. Earning your trident daily demands you bring your wholeness into the world and positively focus it every day.

• • •

There are a lot of nuances packed into this simplified five-step process. We will cover it all in this book.

You are not alone on this new journey — there are many who are following the *Unbeatable Mind* prescription, including athletes, executives, moms, dads, teens, martial artists, yoga practitioners, and spiritual seekers. This book will provide the basic philosophy and tools to allow you to win in your mind, forge grit, and develop an offensive attitude. It will help you to train yourself and your team to peak performance and, more importantly, to lead with your heart and mind merged in action. I encourage you to enjoy the journey rather than focus on the destination. For every mountain you climb and plateau you rest at, there will be another and more interesting view ahead.

UNCOVER YOUR WHY AND POSITIVELY FOCUS IT

CHAPTER ONE

WIN IN THE MIND

"Victorious warriors win first and then go to war, while defeated warriors go to war first and then seek to win."

—Sun Tzu

A month before I tested for my black belt in Seido Karate, I embarked on a final tune-up retreat at the Zen Mountain Monastery in Woodstock, NY, where the Seido team gathered a couple of times a year. Our schedule had us practicing the physical aspects of karate and the mental aspects of Zen in a very yin-yang fashion: Two hours of meditation followed by two hours of karate training, twice a day.

The first morning, as I took my seat on the little bench (which was supposed to take the pressure off our knees and allow us to keep our backs straight), I snuck a peek around. At the monastery that was generous enough to allow us to share their space, most of their students were monks in residence. If you could imagine what a professional meditator looks like, they were in that room. I felt like an intruder and wondered if they could sense the charlatan in the room. After about ten minutes of trying to focus on my breathing, counting each inhale and exhale, I was exhausted, and my back hurt like hell. Why did this suck so much? Where were the peace and bliss I was expecting? Who would have thought that doing nothing could be so acutely painful and hard?

Try harder, I told myself: Concentrate on that spot in front of you. I got to the count of two but realized I was thinking about breakfast. Back to zero. The next determined attempt I made it to the count of three but was vaguely aware that in the back of my mind I was fantasizing about a girl I had met the previous weekend. That's not meditating, I confessed to myself. Back to zero again.

The experience was a real "eye-opener," and it wasn't my third eye that was opening. I could barely make it ten minutes before my mind, like a monkey frantically grasping for a banana, would race off in another direction. I called it "concentration camp" because we were instructed to concentrate on the counting, and it sure felt like a mental prison cell. "Just sit and count your breath," instructed Daido, the head monk. "When the mind wanders, bring it back to the breath. Don't beat yourself up; life is too short." Oddly, life never felt longer…I was used to things being easy and couldn't help beating myself up for sucking so much at a skill that I had imagined would be as easy as stretching out in a hammock.

Despite my clumsiness, I began to register a surprising change. Even though I kept feeling like a meditative failure, I noticed the more I did it, the better I felt. Maybe, I considered, this type of internal work didn't require the aggressive goal orientation of my school sports' training or the general Western mindset that drove me through my work as a CPA. Maybe there was no "there" there. What I ultimately discovered was that even if I sucked at sitting in silence, it worked its magic anyhow. I was circling back to another part of my past: The silence of the bench was not much different than the silence of nature I had enjoyed in my youth. What a simple yet profound discovery!

The major lesson I gained from my journey into Zen, one that I wish to share with you now, was that I could gain control over my mind—if I consistently practiced, practiced holding a true, complete state of silence in the mind. When you achieve this place of silence, only then can you witness the mind in action. In doing so you begin to separate your identity from "the thoughts" and get acquainted with that part of you watching the thoughts. That space between the thought and the watcher—your witness—is where the magic is. Absent that space, efforts to develop concentration, confidence, creativity, and spirit fall light years short.

You, too, must learn to approach mental training without goal orientation. Be patient and expect the unexpected.

Later, as my twenty-year SEAL career unfolded, I sought to understand those seeds that Kaicho Nakamura had planted during those formative years in New York City. I noted that during long training hikes and numbingly long dives, my mind began to drop into the same meditative state I had experienced on the Zen bench. Hours would slip by as a calmness and sense of confidence penetrated my awareness. When a crisis hit, rather than try and intellectualize or instantly think up a route through the problem, I learned to feel my way through crisis moments.

I'd observed how excessive thinking and analysis paralysis had been responsible for injuries and deaths. I chose instead to surrender to my intuition and seek presence in place of constant rationalization. Over time I became vividly aware of what was transpiring in and around me. This present moment mindset centered my rational mind within even more control and allowed for creativity to flow. These experiences piqued my interest in training the inner skills even more. I wondered:

- How could I deepen my intuition?
- Could I learn to activate that precious flow state at will?
- Could I intentionally slow down time and ensure I was calm in the midst of a crisis?
- How were deep breathing, internal visualization, positivity, and effective planning practices linked?
- What impact did these tools have for long-term goal actualization versus spot performances?
- How could I develop my creativity?
- What were the limits to my performance as a human?

In 2006, I was hired by the Navy to train and mentor all SEAL candidates nationwide (an invitation that launched my third business, US Tactical). This program was the driver behind my creating an integrated training program and offering it to the public. That training became the petri dish for developing the principles discussed in these pages. That is where I developed the tactics behind the First Premise.

"SEEING" THE WIN

SEALs operate at an elite level because they know how to discipline their minds and secure the win internally before they enter the fight. This is what I call The First Premise, and we must first go into the belly of this beast to tackle how to develop mental control. You don't have time or the luxury to join a monastery or spend twenty years as a SEAL as I did (unless that is your goal, of course!). For many of you, it will be the first time you have been challenged to think about the mind in the way I will present here. Stay with me, and trust that what I am offering works. After you establish a foundation for mental control, then you can move on to more "practical" concepts in the ensuing chapters.

But where do we start if our minds are like runaway freight trains? For most of us, sitting in silent meditation can seem impossible. With great intentions we give it a try but are immediately frustrated by the busyness and randomness of our mental machinations. Attempts to settle the mind by just sitting and trying not to think can lead to frustration and failure. As a teenager I did Transcendental Meditation™ with my dad for a few days. Sitting in a nice, comfortable chair, I tried like hell to focus on their mantra. My mind conspired to turn this effort into a disaster, as after several seconds my inner dialogue started chattering like a schoolgirl about anything and everything: What's for dinner? Gotta go mow the lawn. Wish I hadn't said that to Sally. Boy, I have a lot of homework to do. What the heck am I doing this for anyway? This sucks…I have too much to do…I'm out of here!

The only consolation prize was that my dad failed miserably, too. We both gave it up. Only later with

Nakamura, did I come to understand how we are bred to identify with our thoughts. This is a critical problem. We find meaning by constantly thinking of our body, beliefs, successes, failures, rules, and roles in life. We have few mechanisms to shut these lines of thought down except for sleep.

As we age and further empower the rational mind, the humble witness weakens in its shadow. We are rarely, if ever, encouraged to spend time in silence or get to know the depth of our character. All the while our souls cry out for attention. But controlling our thoughts can seem counterintuitive. After all, aren't they — our thoughts — us? Heading down this path can be terrifying. What would you become if you disassociated from your thoughts? Fear, frustration, and time demands sidetrack many of us from this penetrating brand of silence, and we quit before we experience the surrender.

If this has been your experience, please know that you aren't alone. My message to you is this: forget about the past and the failed efforts. Take this moment to formally and forever let go and give yourself a fresh start. Now is the only time that matters Getting to the terrain of elite performers demands attaining access to the 90 percent or so of the vast mental power that lies beyond the rational, thinking part of your mind.

Let's break this down and discuss how to go about accomplishing it.

EMBRACING SACRED SILENCE

Sacred silence is the experience of incredible internal peace that accrues when you learn to connect to your "witness" and let go of your ego's cravings and outward reaching for acceptance. It is intrinsically motivating when you begin to experience sacred silence. For most Unbeatable Mind students, this is the turning point from "trying this new thing out" to "committing to a practice for life."

Most meditation practices come from Eastern cultures and are difficult for the contemporary Westerner to wrap their steel-trap heads around. I've watched the eyes of my SEAL trainees glaze over when I've used terms from yoga or the martial arts traditions. To solve this challenge, I took the "fu" out of kung fu and fashioned tools and language more suitable for the Western student. This led to simple drills, such as box breathing, an intrinsic key to success for beginning Unbeatable Mind students that helps us focus to connect with our witness. But what is this witness? I will endeavor to unpack this whale of a concept.

THE WITNESS

Have you ever been knee-deep in an argument and suddenly felt removed, as if you were watching the event from afar? You may have broken out laughing as you shifted from identifying with the words spewing out of your mouth (led by your ego) to what I call your witness.

Those moments are liberating and portend a sea-change in what you think of as your mind. The ability to gain distance from your thoughts and emotions while engaged in "life," allows you to detach from those same thoughts and emotions. This takes us out of reactionary mode and puts us back in control of our internal states. The more you practice connecting with your witness during, for example, box breathing (which I will share with you soon), the more you appreciate that you are not your petty, often negative, thoughts but something much bigger and more eternal. This non-attached witnessing mind creates space for the positive energies of love, forgiveness, creativity, and for abundance to flow, releasing the shackles of negativity and feelings of being less than, and from focusing on what you lack.

When you embark on an Unbeatable Mind meditative practice with discipline, you soon recognize that the witness aspect of your mind has always been there...you just didn't recognize it. You have to slow down and put the constant *doing* on pause to connect with this beingness that is inherent in you. When you ask yourself, *"How do I know I am alive?"* it is your witness that responds. This is your most authentic self, aware of life and the constantly unfolding experience.

I will be unpacking Unbeatable Mind tools throughout this book — though witnessing is not a tool, rather an outcome of the work. Some tools include breathwork for stress management, concentration techniques for attention control, journaling and insight meditation to align your life with your purpose. These and other skills all work synergistically to forge the Unbeatable Mind one day at a time. But when you first begin to polish and still your mind, it is likely you will notice how habitually you harbor weak and negative thoughts. Let's address this first.

STARVING FEAR, FEEDING COURAGE

SEALs are trained to be rock steady and positively focused, but we are no strangers to the twin demons of negative thoughts and feelings. When I checked into SEAL BUD/S Class 170, my nerves were sizzling. I could feel the adrenaline pulsing through my arteries. The instructors had a superhuman quality, and we students were like carpenter ants trying not to be crushed by the big boots hovering above us. The stream of negative, internal chatter in the minds of my fellow trainees was evidenced by the anxiety and dread riddling their faces. I was picking up a lot of it myself, and the fear was manifesting as tension in my stomach. I reached back into my Zen toolbox and decided to redirect my focus away from the fear. I told myself: *I've trained hard. I've made it this far. Many have gone before me and made it. If they did it, so can I. Quitting is not an option. They'll have to kill me to get me out of here!* This positive self-talk became my constant internal companion and a most lethal weapon against the demon of crushing negativity brought on by stress and fear.

When I uttered those words in the comfort of my own mind, I could feel the fear melt away, a firepower of courage replacing it. I had allowed my witness to observe my thoughts and separate from them, and then I took action. I redirected my thoughts and emotions toward a positive focus.

This one skill is a game changer because negativity erodes performance as sure as ocean waves erode the beach. It is imperative to retrain this default mode in our minds — shift it from witnessing negative thoughts to positive, courage-building thoughts. Or, as the Native Americans might say with this vivid, metaphorical punch: starve the fear wolf and feed the courage wolf.

This skill — disengaging from negative thinking and re-directing — is what I call the "WIRM" method. Here is a brief recap:

1. **Witness** the negative thoughts and emotions when they arise (as soon as possible).
2. **Interdict** these negative thoughts by stopping them in their tracks with a powerful countering statement.
3. **Redirect** your mind to a positive focus with self-talk and imagery specific to your current goal.
4. **Maintain** this new mental state with a positive jingle (a mantra) that you run in the background of your mind to ward off the negative patterns from arising again.

Interdiction power statements are words and phrases that shock your negative mind back into your positive control. Words like "no" or "stop" work well in a pinch, but using positive power statements can have more power, such as: "I've got this, easy day." "Piece of cake." "Step it up, Mark." "Feed the courage wolf!" You will want to develop a power statement with some shock force that resonates with you. Then, try to practice using it daily whenever you notice negative thinking, until it becomes second nature. Negative patterns will always return until you train them out…which can take years. However, you will never get rid of them unless you discipline yourself to train your mind. When I note a student going negative in our company's immersive training events, my staff or I will assist them to perform an interdiction. "What wolf are you feeding, Joe? Starve that fear wolf and feed the courage wolf!" The student is temporarily taken out of their mental rut and, in a moment, can choose a new direction, a positive one. But if they lack a solid redirect strategy, they will revert back to the negative rut.

The secret for a successful redirect is to inject a new positive thought into your stilled mind that aligns with your immediate goal. This is where a jingle or mantra plays an invaluable role.

A jingle is a rhyme or saying that is positively charged. It engages your conscious mind with positive words, images, and feelings. "Every day, in every way, I'm getting better and better." That phrase was coined by French Doctor Émile Coué. He was able to heal his patients by having them change negative thinking and emotional states with that simple jingle. I use it myself every day, along with a couple of others.

With practice, your mantra will run like background music in your mind with little or no prodding. It won't prevent you from problem-solving but serve as the gatekeeper for your mind's witness, allowing you to be more present and ward off negativity before it lands. Your jingle will keep your mind under control and unfettered by thoughts and beliefs that can sap your energy and degrade your performance.

Often, I will use this tool when an entire team is suffering from a defeatist attitude. "Hooyah, team. We got this! Let's focus on a positive solution. Feed the courage wolf!" Instructions to this effect can shock a team out of a slump instantaneously. Combined with regular meditative work, starting with Box Breathing (a concentration technique I will introduce you to shortly), you will experience immediate results just by practicing this one vital skill.

Now, to begin the Unbeatable Mind training practices, let's discuss a simple concentration tool to clear your mind.

Exercise 1: The Fishbowl Visualization

The Fishbowl is super-effective because you are developing the skills of concentration, metacognition, and visualization all in one powerful practice. I should explain that the term *meditation* includes a broad array of practices, such as breathwork, concentration, mantra, contemplation, visualization, mindfulness, witnessing, and insight. Even time in nature or a long run can be considered meditation if done with the intention of *witnessing context* as opposed to *thinking content*. Each practice will have a different effect on the brain and development of the mind, and I will be specific with what form we are using.

Anytime we engage in an integrative physical, mental, emotional, intuitive, or spiritual training practice, we call it "doing the work." It is ideal to do the work in the same, distraction-free place every time. Yes, I know this can be challenging if your lifestyle includes travel and a busy homelife. Do your best. Find a comfortable place to sit in a chair, on a cushion, or on a stool. (Google *seiza bench* if that interests you.) The key is to keep your spine straight but avoid discomfort that will disrupt your mind. The best postural practices are:

- knees below your hips
- tailbone pointing toward the ground (hips slightly forward)
- spine straight
- hands either folded in front of the belly or on the knees
- chin slightly tucked and the crown of the head rising toward the ceiling
- shoulders relaxed

- eyes, ideally, slightly open with a 45-degree downward gaze

Your gaze will be soft and unfocused. If that is too distracting, you can shut the eyes. I have meditated with my eyes open and shut, and found it easier to learn with them shut. However, to progress to higher stages of awareness and what is called the "awakened state," you will want to learn to meditate with your eyes open. Thus, there is a benefit to open-eyed meditation from the start. Consider trying different postures to avoid discomfort, which will further distract your mind. Standing is fine for brief periods if your back or knees begin to ache.

OK, now you are ready to clear your mind using the Fishbowl technique. (If this approach doesn't work for you, feel free to try meditating the Zen way. Just sit and count each breath cycle, trying to get to ten, while watching for any errant thoughts. If they arise, note them, release them, go back to zero, and count the breath again.)

• • •

Imagine your skull as a fishbowl and your thoughts are what makes the water in the bowl murky (not too far from the truth, I bet!). Your breathing is the filter. Each deep breath you take in and then exhale, cleans the water. You begin to sense the water of your mind getting clearer as you breathe. After ten breaths, it is mostly clean. After twenty breaths, it is as pure as a natural spring on a sunny day. You are witnessing your mind in a stable state with the only *thought energy* being the visualization that you are holding. In this state, your mind is unspoiled by random thinking or elaborate stories. Maintain this state as long as you can. If you start thinking again, your fishbowl gets dirty, so recommit to cleaning it.

This drill is a great concentration practice in itself or it can be used to prepare for another meditation session. Congrats, you just meditated!

My recommendation is to settle into your silence practice (whether you use the Fishbowl technique or the simpler Zen counting practice) for the next couple of weeks.

If you'd like to be guided by a video, all the practices in this book can be found at our Unbeatable Mind online course: https://unbeatablemind.com.

• • •

In the next chapter, we will dive into basic brain organization and operation to learn how to harness the brain's neuroplastic capabilities. Understanding this foundation will allow us to reprogram its hard-wired biases and unlock our 20X mind power potential.

CHAPTER TWO

TRAINING THE BRAIN ZOO

"If you let cloudy water settle, it will become clear. If you let your upset mind settle, your course will also become clear."

—Gautama Buddha

Whether you lead a multinational corporation or a classroom of unruly kids, you will be more successful by not trusting your monkey brain and learning to use your mind more expansively. There are tools to train both — which will streamline and improve your decisions. This chapter introduces core practices to develop the brain and mind to access the "whole mind" and utilize decision models to speed up and improve decision making, break patterns of biased, one-dimensional thinking, and avoid groupthink, procrastination, and analysis paralysis. It is fairly easy to be clever, but it takes a lot of work to become wise.

THE BRAIN ZOO

I wish I had a dollar for every time I put my foot in my mouth from jumping to a conclusion utterly devoid of truth or from operating out of some type of bias. I bet I am not alone here. Eventually, I stopped trusting my above average, rational brain to make good decisions. I recommend you do the same! If you google *cognitive bias*, a concept introduced in 1972 by Nobel Laureate Daniel Kahneman pops up, along with a helpful graphic designed by John Manoogian III called the Cognitive Bias Codex. It categorizes over 100 of the most common biases that arise from four basic conditions:

1. having too much information
2. not having enough meaning
3. needing to act fast
4. deciding (inaccurately) what should be remembered

The untrained brain deploys mental shortcuts to save time and energy. In some cases, they are useful but, in most, they lead to suboptimal decisions. The human brain is a vastly complex and powerful tool but is still little understood beyond the basic building blocks and their plausible functions. The Western view equates the "thinking brain" with "the mind." This is a limited understanding. A more accurate view is that mind exists independent of the brain but requires the brain to communicate and perceive the material world, just as it requires the rest of the body to move and get shit done. This is an important point to reinforce: Unbeatable Mind training is meant to optimize the physical brain's functioning (working memory, mental flexibility, and self-control). Additionally, it teaches trainees to tap into the intelligence of the heart, gut, and nervous system — to access the direct perceiving power of the mind, to learn independent of the physiological brain. Once we achieve this level of awareness, we can then operate from the whole mind. To ground our discussion, I will give a brief overview of the brain and mind before elaborating further.

The reptilian brain is formed from the brain stem and cerebellum. This is our oldest brain. It is almost identical to a reptile's whole brain, hence the name. The reptilian brain regulates basic life functions like breathing, heart rate, and respiration (functions of the brain stem), balance, posture, and movement coordination (the cerebellum). It is also responsible for hardwiring behaviors from memories, which is where deeply rooted training information is stored and retrieved. It may also be safe to assume that this brain is a component of the subconscious mind.

The mammalian brain evolved some 300 million years ago. It is called the mammalian brain because it is similar to the most evolved part of all mammals' brains. The prominent behaviors it regulates are the fight, flight, or freeze response and our need to feed and reproduce. It is also responsible for emotional behavior and regulating chemical and hormonal activity. When you get depressed, you can blame the mammalian brain. But you can then thank it for regulating your body temperature, blood sugar levels, digestion, hormonal balance, and other important things.

The mammalian brain houses the pituitary gland, which is the master hormone gland, and the pineal gland, which regulates sleep. It also includes the hippocampus, which is your memory sorting and storing tool, and the amygdala, which sifts and filters incoming information for threats and opportunities. This sub-brain is largely responsible for the bias toward negativity, which is so prominent in the human condition (discussed earlier in Chapter One). The fear wolf spends most of his time lurking here, sending fear signals to the third sub-brain.

The third sub-brain, the monkey brain, is the most recent addition to the zoo and the seat of awareness, cognition, problem solving, and creativity. It is more properly called the neocortex and is the *command center*, where we reason, plan, intellectualize, analyze, verbalize, and learn. It allows us to interpret events and react to them accordingly. This new brain of ours is so complex it would be an injustice to try and summarize it here. When someone says you are operating out of *right-brain* or *left-brain* thinking, they are referring to the hemispheres of the neocortex. This part of our brain differentiates us from other mammals and is one of the reasons why the human brain has such enormous potential. The frontal lobe of the neocortex is your *executive office*, where intent, focus, and willpower conspire to move you toward greatness or misery. In your teen years, this area is not yet fully developed, which brings clarity to many of the hard-to-explain decisions you made in adolescence, a period well-tended to by your emotional mammalian brain.

Now, it makes sense that these many "animals" in your head need a zookeeper to keep them in line. Who does that job? Here's a thought: How about your witness? Let's consider the mind — as in consciousness — itself. This is what I referred to earlier as the witness. The witness exists independent of the organ of the brain. Certain scientists and philosophers like to reduce the mind and consciousness to correlates of chemical releases and electrical firings in the brain. Feel free to openly laugh at this notion. Whatever you do, don't believe them for a minute. These are simply neurological byproducts of the mind accessing memories, imagining, perceiving, dreaming, thinking, and feeling. Your experience of a conscious mind certainly has chemical and electrical correlates, but it is a mistake to define consciousness as mere brain electrochemical signaling.

Studies of near-death and out-of-body experiences support this idea. The yogis and various spiritual, Eastern traditions believe that the mind is consciousness, and consciousness is one's unique soul using the organs of thinking and feeling (the brain, heart, belly, nervous, and neuroendocrine systems) to make meaning and create your reality. The mind not only has its own unique imprint (like a fingerprint of the soul), it makes meaning from the collective stimuli of life experiences and has an interconnection to other beings and to a universal intelligence, the latter being that vast spirit that runs through all things. So, if the mystics are to be believed (and science is proving them right every day), then consciousness transcends, though includes, the matter and functions of the brain itself. But an untrained brain-mind is like an untrained body — weak, lethargic, and not very functional.

To connect with and control this intricate mind, you must train your neocortex to acknowledge that it isn't the only animal in town, and it isn't in charge. Only then can your witness get back in the seat to become the zookeeper and direct the activities of the mind-brain. The problem is that we have largely denied the witness in our culture. Instead, we identify almost exclusively with thoughts in our brain as our primary and accurate source of information. The thinker, the neocortex, doesn't want to give up this "anointed" position. Moreover, the neocortex is like a wild monkey — it's powerful and brimming with potential but also dangerous and remarkably unproductive until trained. It is restless, running from pain, chasing pleasure, and fiercely resistant to any attempts at restraint for training purposes.

We discussed earlier how martial artists, yogis, and monks learned long ago that they could train the monkey mind through concentration and sacred silence methods such as meditation. When they did this, they achieved a merging with the witness (soul) and a taming of the thinking mind (ego). They could then operate from their witnessing self, while focusing their thinking minds with precision on the selected subject or object of attention.

If this all sounds too esoteric, I can simplify. This merging is not unlike the peak experience you have in a moment of flow when you're highly skilled in a specific domain, such as is a SEAL, first responder, or elite athlete in action. In that moment of laser-like intensity and challenge, the mind operates from an unhindered witness, time seems to collapse to the "now," and you are thrust into what feels like a state of flow. In these moments, the frontal lobe of the neocortex is so focused on the object of attention that any other thoughts are forced out, allowing the unfettered direct perception of the witness to target the object or action. As mentioned, in this state, the constructs of time and space seem to loosen their grip on the mind. In this manner, the trained frontal lobe becomes your "flow activator," dissolving past and future into the present moment. Training so that you can activate the flow state at will takes time and patience. The witness process for mental control and sacred silence practices that I describe in this book are the best ways that I know of to accomplish this training — and are key focuses of the Unbeatable Mind Academy. As soon as you begin training, you will note that the animals running amok in your mind take notice and line up. They become a support team for your witness, instead of fighting against it.

As if the distracting chatter of the untrained monkey mind isn't enough to make you anxious, the way the neocortex interacts with the mammalian and reptilian brains is also a cause for concern. In 2011, economist and Nobel Prize winner Daniel Kahneman wrote an intriguing book about how the mind works in decision-making. The book *Thinking, Fast and Slow* provides deep insight into the tricks our animal brains play on us. Kahneman wondered how much control the neocortex really had over our thoughts and actions, or whether the older brains had a say.

His central theme is that there are two primary modes of thought. The first (which he calls System 1) is the instinctual (fast) and emotional thought process driven by your mammalian and reptilian brains. The second (System 2) is deliberate (slow), rational, and logical cognition driven by the neocortex. System 1 is constantly monitoring the environment as well as your inner space to form down-and-dirty impressions. It probes for information important to survival and reproduction and calmly takes care of routine business — until it detects a threat or opportunity. Then, it perks up and mobilizes the executive offices in the neocortex to activate System 2 and figure things out with more detail.

This is where the challenge arises — in the dynamic interplay between the two systems.

Nowadays, thanks to the extraordinary amount of information flowing in from external and internal sources, System 1 must make assumptions and take shortcuts. Add to this the inherent laziness of System 1 (after all, it must save energy for the inevitable crisis), and you end up with knee-jerk reactions and hair-trigger responses that turn out to be dead wrong more often than not. The shortcuts and guesswork made sense in the old days — for detecting a saber-tooth tiger or capturing the heart of the cave girl next door — but in today's world they can cause trouble.

To compensate, the brain will associate new information to the closest other idea, which then primes your answer. This *priming effect* leads to one of the more common errors of perception called *confirmation bias*, made famous by Malcolm Gladwell in his book, *Blink*. (More on him in a bit.) This process goes mostly undetected, but the effects are obvious when you stop and look. An example Kahneman provides is if you have recently seen or heard the word *eat*, you are more likely to complete the word fragment so_p as *soup*. However, if you just got out of the bath, you would be primed to read the word fragment as *soap*.

Kahneman describes an experiment in a company kitchen where an honesty box is used to pay for coffee. A picture of a flowerpot was hung in the room for a stint, and then changed out for a portrait. The employees contributed almost three times as much when the eyes in the portrait were watching. This was due to the priming effect!

Consider this sentence: Ann approached the bank. If you are a city dweller, you conjured up an image of Ann walking toward an ATM. But, if you're a river guide, you would be primed to see Ann glide up to the riverbank in her kayak. When you buy a red Mazda, isn't it amazing how your mind confirms that practically everyone else suddenly owns a red car and there seems to be twice as many Mazdas on the road? How can we trust our minds when this type of gross misinterpretation is going on all the time?

Let's look at our proclivity to jump to conclusions with bias. System 1 works only with the information that it has ready access to. When evaluating people, System 1 is inclined to stereotype because, if no other information is available, that is the only pathway we have to conjure an instant impression. This gave us an edge in the past, but that edge has long dulled. In one study, psychologist Solomon Asch, a pioneer in social psychology in the twentieth century, asked subjects to describe two hypothetical characters, Alan and Ben. Here are the descriptions of the two: Alan — intelligent, industrious, impulsive, critical, stubborn, envious; Ben — envious, stubborn, critical, impulsive, industrious, intelligent. As you may have noticed, the descriptors are identical but for their order of delivery. Subjects consistently rated Alan favorable to Ben because the initial traits in the list impacted their first impression. The *halo effect*, where you transfer a trait such as good looks onto character when there is no other evidence to support the notion, is another manifestation of the priming effect of System 1.

Sales professionals are familiar with another mind trick called *framing*. How information is framed affects how it is processed. My friend, Oren Klaff, bestselling author of *Pitch Anything*, teaches the use of framing to help entrepreneurs pitch for financing. They typically have great success by breaking pre-established frames for a temporary edge. This sounds all very Machiavellian, but I am 100 percent certain that I have fallen for it myself.

A final example of how System 1 distorts System 2 thinking is with *loss aversion* (and one that I had painful experiences with during the 2001 dot-com bust). The System 1 mammalian brain sees losses as a threat and will avoid them at the expense of gains. After all, threats are more urgent than opportunities. Consider the following example: You are offered a gamble on the toss of a coin. If the coin shows tails, you lose $100. If the coin shows heads, you win $150. Is this gamble attractive? Would you accept it? Rationally, it's good because the expected value is positive. But most people reject this gamble because the fear of losing $100 is more intense than the hope of gaining $150. This loss aversion comes into play in all forms of negotiations. Since losses are felt more keenly than gains, the side that stands to lose will fight harder against it. It is also prevalent when it comes to cutting investment losses, which is why we tend to hold onto a losing stock. Selling it actualizes the loss. Whole-mind thinking cuts through bias and slows down internal time, so you can focus more clearly. Then, you'll be able to employ mental models to streamline the decision-making processes, which we will discuss in Chapter Eight.

SHORTCUTTING THE GLADWELL EFFECT

Now that I have dumped liberally on the human brain for its shortcomings, I wonder how we can shore it up for better decision-making. In his book, *Blink: The Power of Thinking Without Thinking*, Malcolm Gladwell introduces us to the concept of *mental intuition*, which is gained through deep expertise or immersion into an area of great interest. Gladwell tells us that those who master a skill, whether it be chess, basketball, or firefighting, are able to respond intuitively to a situation at a glance. The chess or basketball moves flow spontaneously and are almost always strong and creative. The firefighter, who has a sudden urge to escape a burning house just before it collapses, senses the danger intuitively.

Gladwell posits that expertise at this level is formed from the intersection of deep knowledge, experience that leads to expert skill, and being present. So, based on what we've learned about the brain so far, we can assert that this intuitional expertise is developed in the mammalian brain, which unconsciously picks up nuanced cues and sends them to the neocortex (System 2) at opportune moments for advantage. These actions are then perceived as heroic or genius or superhuman in some cases. Since the mammalian brain has been well primed to look for nuances, those are now available to the thinking part of your brain and show up as insights. The neocortex, when trained or naturally in a present state of awareness, will be able to interpret these messages easily.

Now, according to Gladwell, the capacity for this type of unconscious intuitive behavior takes years to hone — at least ten thousand hours of practice. But here's what I find fascinating: Gladwell's assertions are based on a "common," untrained mind. (Yes, intuition can arise due to deep concentration on a narrow set of skills over a long period of time.) I believe this type of behavior can be accelerated greatly when we train as I offer in this book. My premise is that when we actively engage in training the whole mind-body-spirit system, rather than shaping each gradually or haphazardly, we are able to access the same level of genius that Gladwell speaks of in shorter periods of time. My experience in the SEALs and with my trainees has proven this is possible, though scientific validation may be lacking as of this writing.

A word of caution: though intuitive genius is a worthy goal, you must still use a two-pronged approach to training. As you train your mind, you can't necessarily ignore your neocortex — which houses a wealth of accumulated knowledge — or the intuitive inspiration you receive may be flawed. You may not see the whole picture. This presents an awkward paradox: Do you trust your gut implicitly? Or do you use it as a guide while seeking external validation? Perhaps the setting will dictate. In an existential crisis, you will need to trust your gut. In a multimillion-dollar business deal, it's a good idea to trust...then verify.

SEALs safeguard against this by using mental systems to better frame and back up their decisions. Models like this provide an insurance policy against the zoo-brain's tricks and traps.

Exercise 2: Journaling

Journaling is an excellent way to sew your insights into the thoughts, ideas, fears, desires, and dreams that come up during concentration and meditation work. When you journal, you will observe patterns in your thinking. Further, the act of writing is exercise for the brain. Research says the use of the opposable thumb is directly related to the development of our neocortex. A journaling habit is a great way to reflect while sharpening your mental powers! I recommend you take up journaling to record your reflections during our mental training sessions.

Please take five minutes or so to practice the Zen counting or the Fishbowl visualization technique. Then, journal about the experience, any thoughts or feelings that arose to help or hinder your focus.

• • •

In the next chapter, we'll talk about using your new positive focus skills to develop emotional resiliency, which will give you the foundation to forge mental toughness and an unbeatable mind.

CHAPTER THREE

EMOTIONAL RESILIENCY

"Life doesn't get easier or more forgiving, we get stronger and more resilient."

—Steve Maraboli, *Life, the Truth, and Being Free*

When I was younger, I was a great daydreamer. But, if you had asked me to describe what my future looked like, what my purpose was, or what my principles were, I would have responded with a blank stare. This lack of awareness caused me much hand-wringing and lost time but, to be fair, most young people aren't clear on their purpose. What about adults? I've often wondered how many grownups are in the same boat I was back in my teens. People in their forties, fifties, and later in life — do they lack this kind of clarity? The inability to see and articulate a future full of purpose, passion, and principles was cured by my Zen training with Kaicho Nakamura. Yours will be cured by doing the work in the next three chapters.

THE 3Ps AND YOUR ONE THING

It's crucial to have enough self-awareness so you can articulate your 3Ps and your One Thing. Let's look at these by asking a few questions:

1. What am I *passionate* about and how can I do more of that?
2. What do I value, and how can I develop these *principles*, so they define my character for the rest of my life?
3. What is my *purpose*? Who am I and what am I here for?

Once you understand your 3Ps, you can then ask:

1. What is the *one thing* I am supposed to accomplish in my life, and what does that mean for me right now?

Mastery over the self is difficult if you don't have clarity on these questions. If you don't know yourself, what are you supposed to do besides just get by? After all, lack of meaning and purpose is a major cause of despair and despondency in the world. A miniscule number of people have their purpose shown to them early in life and are well into fulfilling it by their twenties. A small but greater percentage stumble upon a vague sense of purpose in their professional lives — fate was kind to them — and they dance around it, feeling sort of OK most days. They have a "this could be worse" attitude about life, which isn't the greatest but…could be worse. But the lion's share of folks never gets a taste of why they're here or the direction in which they should be traveling. I've found this with my students. Most cannot clearly articulate their purpose and are deeply moved when they do the work and uncover it. Now that we're clear on the 3Ps, let's look at your One Thing.

It's likely you have a sense of your own uniqueness, that aspect that sets you apart from others. This uniqueness is coded into your DNA, and I believe it's part of your soul's yoking to your physical body. Regardless of your philosophical or religious orientation, you may sense that your soul whispers to your mind. It speaks of your deepest yearnings and has, resultingly, propelled you in surprising directions throughout your life. If you've ignored this voice in the past, my guess is you've felt out of sorts and misaligned by some decisions, as I did in my early twenties, working as a CPA. Listening to your inner voice will help you define your 3Ps and lead you to your One Thing. Then you can align them with your actions and march forth with confidence and peace of mind.

You've already been introduced to some methods for stilling your monkey mind and creating space for insight and guidance to arise. Shortly, we will start to uncover your 3Ps and One Thing by asking deeply personal questions in layers. First, let's talk about the foundation of mental toughness.

EMOTIONAL RESILIENCY

How many times have you let your emotions torpedo a relationship or stressful project? Do you fly off the handle with your kids or significant other, then reel yourself back in with an excuse or apology? We've all been there.

Resiliency is the ability to bounce back from any setback—physical, mental, or emotional. Emotional resiliency takes patience and courage to develop but it's an imperative skill and the foundation on which mental toughness stands. Here's how to become resilient:

1. **Witness** the negative emotional reaction.
2. **Interdict** it with a power statement that stops it in its track.
3. **Observe** the root emotion beneath it.
4. **Lean** into that root emotion to experience it fully, ensuring that you are avoiding denial or transference.
5. **Transmute** the negative emotional energy to its positive correlate. (Fear can be focused into courage; anger into commitment; jealousy into appreciation; and the most devastating emotion, shame, can become pride, while despair becomes surrender.)
6. **Engage** the new emotion with imagery and positive self-talk that supports it and blocks the old emotion from re-emerging.
7. **Take Action.** Of course, that action may require you to take your eyes off yourself to focus on a teammate.

The positive momentum you develop from mastering emotional resiliency will take you to a new, more productive and emotionally balanced level in all areas of your life.

Let me walk you through a personal example of emotional resilience in action.

During Operation Iraqi Freedom, I was quoted in a newspaper article — with a provocative title about the

SEALs—about some losses that occurred. In my opinion, the SEALs were being employed to do conventional unit jobs in broad daylight, in contradiction to our doctrine of being the silent warriors who operated at night and were gone before the enemy knew what hit them. The author of the article, without my approval, used my reserve officer rank in the story, making the comment appear semiofficial. I got called on the carpet by a SEAL captain who read me the riot act.

As I stood tall in front of this man, I felt anger rising. My instinctual response was to fight back by lashing out. In the military, if you're getting dressed down, you shut up and take it. Shouting back would have been a serious breach of military protocol and discipline. Because I had trained to connect with my witness and not my reactionary mind, I gained a little distance and observed the scene. I instantly realized that I hadn't been in a situation like this for a long time and that it could be a powerful learning opportunity. Then, I interdicted my emotional response with a "stop" and observed my inner emotional state without losing control, all while getting railed.

Beneath my anger was fear. *What if I get kicked off the team? What if the people I respect hear this version of events and lose respect for me? What if my career goes down the drain because of this misstep?* I recognized the root emotion as a fear of loss. I also saw that I had an issue with authority. To put it bluntly, I felt a lack of trust in this guy. But that was my issue not his.

I made the conscious decision to convert my anger toward this authority figure and the fear of potential loss into a forceful resolution to maintain a positive and professional attitude. I began to envision myself as a well-respected officer, admired for not being afraid to speak up regardless of the consequences. Fortunately, because I was able to connect with my witnessing self and gain that critical distance from my thinking and feeling self, I was able to examine my reaction, kick its tires, and let the captain rage on about what a bad SEAL I was. After all, he was just doing his job and working with the tools that had supported him well in that system.

As you probably predicted, I survived the incident without too much blood loss, and was able to refine my emotional resiliency toolkit. As it turned out, many SEALs and other vets thanked me for what I'd said in the article because they agreed with me in principle and felt the issues needed to be aired so a dialogue could be had. Ultimately, my reputation was enhanced with those who mattered most.

BIG 4 of EMOTIONAL RESILIENCY

These four add up to Emotional Resiliency

THE BIG FOUR OF EMOTIONAL RESILIENCY

It is much easier to be resilient when the Four Attitudes of Emotional Resiliency are burned into your character. Self-esteem is the emotional state of feeling worthy and respected by others. Low self-esteem can come from childhood abandonment, volatile environments where your voice is not heard, or outright abuse. If these attributes exist in your consciousness, get therapeutic help and go deep into the silence practices to taste the underlying goodness inside yourself.

Self-control is the ability to control expressing emotions and desires during challenging situations. Can you imagine the outcome of the scene with my captain had I not practiced self-control?

Have a positive mindset. When you're optimistic, your conscious and subconscious mind view obstacles and setbacks as opportunities — whereas a negative disposition believes all is lost. You're able to bounce back and persevere with the power of positive thinking, which enhances your resiliency.

Finally, resiliency is assured if you have the attitude of being oriented toward others versus yourself. Put yourself in someone else's shoes to understand where they're coming from. If you're service oriented, this attribute comes naturally, and you tend to be a more emotionally resilient person. Viktor Frankl describes this effect in his book, *Man's Search for Meaning*, which chronicles his experiences in a Nazi concentration camp. Viktor survived by finding meaning through tending to the needs of others over his own, and then teaching the power of this simple truth.

This is informed by a robust certainty of your *why*.

Your purpose is the reason you are here. Imagine your purpose as the force behind your life — it is your foundational reason for being on this Earth. My purpose is to master myself, so I can serve humanity as a warrior, leader, and teacher. Your *one thing* is something specific you are working toward today and into the near future that falls under the umbrella of your purpose. (You have many "one things" throughout your life — they keep changing as you do.) Your *why* is your motivation for working toward your *one thing* daily.

At one time, my *one thing* was to earn the trident and become a Navy SEAL. I pushed myself to the brink to earn my SEAL Trident every day, becoming Honor Man of my training class and a respected officer. Why? So I could fulfill my purpose as a warrior leader, effectively serving my team in dangerous times and places, which fed into serving my country. Within the teams, my One Thing was to become the best special operations officer I could. Later on, my One Thing became to train and inspire a new generation of warriors from the ranks of military and civilians alike. The point is that your *why* is like the inner core of the sun, a fusion reactor that keeps you going day in and day out as you pursue each *one thing* on track with your higher purpose.

Sometimes in a crisis we have to narrow our focus, momentarily set aside our commitment to that broader purpose and find a new *why* and *one thing* to survive.

When climber Aron Ralston (profiled in the movie *127 Hours*) found himself alone in the desert, literally stuck between a rock and a hard place, he figured out a way to break his arm and use the dull blade of a multi-tool to amputate it to survive. Aron's purpose is to inspire people through extreme, challenging, physical endeavors. However, in that instance, his *one thing* was to see his unborn daughter. Why? Because he's her father and parenting is one of our strongest motivators for doing anything.

Aron's *why* propelled him to do something most of us could not imagine. His action was successful. He survived and went on to raise daughter and fulfill a higher purpose as an inspirational speaker. The lesson here is that to be emotionally resilient, it is crucial to know your motivation at all times. Know your purpose. Know your *one thing*. Know your *why*. It can make the difference between life and death.

To conclude this chapter, let's start with the Fishbowl visualization technique or Zen counting practice — reader's choice!

After five to ten minutes or longer if you desire, once your mind is still and positively focused, move on to the journal exercise.

Exercise 3: Defining Your 3Ps and Your One Thing

These are good, layered questions to reflect on and journal about as part of your process for defining your passion, principles, and purpose, which lead to your *one thing*:

Your Passion:

• What are you passionate about in a way that defines who you are?

- What makes you feel as if your hair is on fire (besides a fire)?
- What unique skills or talents do you have that you love to use and that make you feel different?
- If you won the lottery today, what would you do differently?

Your Principles:

- What is it that you truly value in your life?
- How can you move toward those things you truly value and away from the things you don't value as much?
- What do these values say about what you are passionate about?
- Do these values point to an overarching purpose in life?
- Can you make a habit of the big, positive values so they become part of your character and then your destiny?

Your Purpose and your One Thing:

- What have you been conditioned to think you are supposed to do with your life?
- What do you think you are really supposed to do with your life?
- What do you feel you are really supposed to do with your life?
- Is there a tiny voice of doubt suggesting you are on the wrong track?

- Is that same voice nudging you forward with the sensation that you are on the right track?
- What *one thing* do you think you are here for? What *one thing* would you focus on if you had nothing holding you back?
- What would you do differently if you knew you had one year to live?

Looking inward and writing down what comes up in a free-flowing manner gets you into an ideal state for the intuitive and creative aspects of your mind to be heard. The exercises in *Unbeatable Mind* will train your mind to enter these intuitive states on demand and, as you do, your insights will deepen even further.

Now that you've articulated your 3Ps and your *one thing* and etched them in stone (in a journal or a Word.doc or in an app on your phone), make sure to review them daily. (Mine are on my smartphone in Notepad.)

● ● ●

Now that you understand what it takes to be emotionally resilient and have a clear focus on your path to self-mastery, let's talk about the greatest components to forging mental toughness: breath control, concentration, and the power of choice.

CHAPTER FOUR

MENTAL TOUGHNESS

"One of the mind's most marvelous qualities is that it can be transformed."

— His Holiness the 14th Dalai Lama

Often, I see people with great minds and all the right stuff for success torpedo themselves on the one-yard line. They do this because they lack mental toughness. As mental control through breathwork is the starting point for an unbeatable mind, mental toughness is what sees you through to the finish line.

Here's the Big Four of Mental Toughness broken down for you:

1. **Breath Control**: using deep breathing to manage stress and the arousal response (fight, flight, or freeze).
2. **Mental Control**: learning to focus your mind and redirect it through positive self-dialogue.

3. **Visualization**: using imagery to ensure your mental picture is mission focused and aimed toward victory. (More on this in Chapter Six.)

4. **Goal Setting**: learning to set, target, and accomplish specific objectives and knowing how to scale them down to micro goals when the going gets tough. (More on this in Chapter Eight.)

THE BIG 4 OF MENTAL TOUGHNESS

Breathe In...
Breathe Out...
Stay Calm!

BREATH (arousal) CONTROL
stress management

MENTAL CONTROL
Control Positive Inner Dialogue

VISUALIZE SUCCESS
Win in your mind first!

GOAL SETTING
S.M.A.R.T - F.I.T.S & Micro Goals

You've already learned how to focus, breathe to still the mind and calm the body, and redirect your negative thoughts to starve your monkey mind and feed positivity — two of the big four skills of mental toughness. In Chapter Three, we learned about the disciplines that create emotional resiliency, the foundation for mental toughness. This is all great news. In this chapter, I will share three of my top secrets for mental toughness.

Prior to starting your journey, things just seemed to happen. Life was random, and you often felt out of control and aimless. Now that you're learning how to focus and redirect your mind, you're back in the driver's seat. You will be able to create exactly what you desire and avoid what you don't. You're writing the script of your own masterpiece: your life.

That life is created from thousands of small decisions made every day. We tend to focus on a few big choices when we reflect on our life experience, some of the common biggies: college, career, marriage, kids, your location of residence when you're born, and when you retire, to name a few. But think about it: Isn't it true that every life-altering choice is a result of all the small decisions you made up to that point?

Let's consider the college example in finer detail. Perhaps as a kid you chose to embrace school rather than resist it. You sought to learn, did your homework, and got decent grades. The daily commitment led to the choice to go to a top university. Alternatively, maybe you resisted school and sometimes didn't even show up. Then, as you approached the end of the process, you had different choices — to get your diploma and find a minimum wage job or go to a community college. Very few decisions you made throughout your formative years had anything to do with your general intelligence or aptitude—yet they broadened or narrowed opportunities moving into adulthood, impacting your life.

Consider this: In your formative years, you chose to embrace fitness and good nutrition. Every day, you asked yourself whether this food or that action would make you more or less healthy. You made a habit of training your body and eating well. Then, in your mid-twenties, you decided to follow your calling to be a Navy SEAL. Because your choices to that point were in alignment with the big decision of becoming a SEAL, you sailed through the program. The alternate universe is obvious, and I don't need to describe what happens to the vast majority of people who make poor choices. Our healthcare, medical, and insurance industries pull in trillions as a result of generations of people making chronic, unhealthy choices in the areas of fitness and nutrition.

OK, so where am I going with this? It's simple. Success is defined by choice, and it's the small decisions, not the major ones, that make the difference between average and excellent.

The first secret to mental toughness is to recognize and embrace the power of choice and respect how it shapes your life. And, perhaps, one of the biggest choices you must learn to make is how you think about, and deal with, stress, because this affects your behavior—all the micro choices you make—every day.

UNDERSTANDING AND MANAGING STRESS

In July of 2008, in Encinitas, California, forty-nine hours and forty-five minutes into the 50-hour Kokoro Camp 7 event, my instructors descended on the class. Kokoro Camp is voluntary, but it's our job to help the trainees discover what's holding them back from greatness and give them the tools to break through to the next stage in their development.

We were on the verge of securing the class when some unspoken urge struck us to press harder. We ratcheted up the intensity and put the class under a whole new level of mental duress by telling them we were tacking on three more hours. To our surprise, one of the trainees up and quit. The new and unexpected stress had unhinged him. He stepped aside. He was done, game over.

A few minutes later, he stared in stunned disappointment from the sideline as we secured the class. We had no plans of going longer — we were gauging mental toughness. He reacted emotionally with his thinking mind. The other fifty-some students either interdicted their negative emotional reaction to the news and made the choice to keep going, or they were still weighing their options when we wrapped.

Stress is so often cited as the cause of poor health, emotional collapse, and failure. The prevailing view in society is that we are helpless victims of stress. How often do you think these thoughts or say them out loud?

- "I am so stressed out."
- "I can't take this stress for one more minute."
- "This job is killing me."

- "I need a (fill in your favorite vice here: drink, smoke, etc.)."

It's a myth that stress is your problem. Your real problem is believing that stress is the source of your woes. In my early twenties, I was there. I know how stress feels, and how easy it is to fall into the victim mentality trap. Now that you know your mind can be your friend or foe, you see how your reaction to stress becomes a story you tell yourself. But you can make a different choice, which will impact your future. To change your story about stress, let's use WIRM, the four-step process you learned, to rethink our reaction to it:

1. **Witness** the adverse stressor as it impacts you and begins to affect your psychology and physiology.
2. **Interdict** the response to the stress.
3. **Redirect** your psychology and physiology to counter the impact of the stress and transmute it to positive performance.
4. **Maintain** performance through breathing and concentration techniques to eliminate the stress from your mind, body, and life.

With this method, you take back control and move from stress to success!

Stress is neither good nor bad, but it gets a bad rap. Most folks think the secret to health and happiness is to eliminate or avoid stress. Good luck. That's like peeing into the wind and not expecting to get wet. Everyone faces stress daily. If we manage it well, we win. If we don't, we suffer. Besides, we need these forces to grow as humans.

Stress is another word for pressure or resistance. Let's use strength training as an example. Lifting weights introduces external resistance stress to our bodies. We must break down old tissues that were programmed for a previous skill level and load and rebuild them if we want more strength and stamina. This is how muscles develop. Most people don't react to this form of physical stress negatively — in fact, scientists call this *eustress*. Eustress is good stress. Heck, after a workout we even call the pain from tearing our muscles a "good sore," and we're happy. But in reality, stress just "is," and we've mentally framed the physical stress of a tough workout as positive and work stress as negative or *distress*.

Here's how this all works: Our brains are wired to process incoming information through the amygdala, located in the temporal lobes of the brain. This information is screened for threats and opportunities. The amygdala interprets many modern influences as threats. The pressure of a work deadline, for example, is identified as a danger, even though a PowerPoint presentation that's due on Thursday is a joke compared to being chased by a cave lion like our ancestors endured. When a threat is detected, the amygdala initiates the fight, flight, or freeze response (also called the hyperarousal or acute stress response). This activates the hypothalamic, pituitary, and adrenal glands, which flood us with adrenaline and cortisol, leading to various familiar physiological effects such as: elevated heart rate, increased blood pressure, rapid breathing, and a boost of energy. You're charged up and ready to launch a right hook or sprint down the street. The physiological changes give the body increased strength and speed. This is a good thing—when we actually need it. But the fight-or-flight response is an adaptive reaction, and negative physiological and psychological effects occur over time from overuse. Prolonged stress responses may also result in chronic suppression of the immune system, leaving the body open to infections.

The stress response can also be activated by the memory of an event or a catastrophic misinterpretation of bodily sensations in the case of post-traumatic stress disorder and panic disorder. My point: our body doesn't care if stress is physical, emotional, real, or conjured up from a memory, it reacts in the same way, and it's up to our brain to manage it.

My four-step process works whether it's to manage one-time acute stress, like in a crisis, or long-term chronic stress, such as the crushing load of commitments.

Incidentally, the main cause of stress in most our lives is self-induced—from lack of time. Redefining your storied relationship with time will reduce a big source of stress in your life. Take on fewer commitments so you can focus more positive energy on what matters and aligns with your purpose. Combine this with the skills I'm about to teach you and watch your performance skyrocket.

DOUBLE-BARREL POWER: BREATHING AND CONCENTRATION

On a mission in 1995, the SEAL Delivery Vehicle (SDV) was cruising along at a depth of twenty-five feet below the surface of the waters off Oahu, Hawaii. I was in the navigator seat, and the more experienced enlisted SEAL was piloting. We were two hours into a five-hour dive mission when water gushed around my face and filled my wraparound breathing apparatus. I could breathe but was blind and disoriented. I fumbled through the standard operating procedures to clear the mask, but it had ruptured and was useless. I reached for my backup mask, but it was nowhere to be found. *Dang.* Somehow, I had lost it on insertion. I immediately understood what the old-timers meant when they said of our equipment: "Two is one, one is none." For the next three hours, I had to deal with the misery of a flooded face mask and of being a helpless bystander as the other SEAL took over piloting and navigation.

So, after the initial fear and frustration wore off, I reverted to my training and settled in for the long and uncomfortable ride. I slowed my breathing, and I began to hold my breath at the inhale and exhale (which I will teach you how to do shortly). I also started to repeat a positive mantra, which deepened my concentration. I was just getting good at all this when the SDV came to a sudden halt, and I got a squeeze on the arm from the pilot. I thought we had a problem but, to my surprise, we had arrived at our destination! Three hours had passed in what felt like forty-five minutes. Rather than feeling stressed out and miserable, I felt peaceful. This was another powerful anchoring experience for just how valuable these skills are.

Without the breathing and concentration skills, I could have panicked and compromised the mission. At minimum, I would have been consumed by the torture of not being able to see. Through my own training and from helping thousands of special operations candidates, I have found that stress of any kind is easily managed with breathing and concentration tools. Yoga practitioners have used breathing and concentration techniques for thousands of years to dissipate stress, develop optimal health, and drive toward spiritual advancement. Breathing is free medicine, and the daily practice of breath control decreases stress and leads to optimal health and a longer life.

Don't wait for a crisis to get started. Learn to breathe and concentrate properly now. It's an accessible technique that leads to true mental toughness.

CONCENTRATION THROUGH BREATHWORK

Deep, long, unbroken, and inspired concentration is a hallmark skill of super-successful people and the second secret to mental toughness. We all understand what it means to concentrate, but can we really do this with enough depth that all distractions are eliminated? Can we concentrate on our *one thing* — the most important thing — with a hair-on-fire intensity until our task is accomplished? Yes, we can. But the only way to improve concentration is by — you guessed it — practicing.

There are many ways to practice concentration. In fact, we have discussed a few already (such as the Fishbowl technique and Zen counting practice). Most of what passes for meditation in the West today, where time is dedicated to focusing on a very narrow range of things or just one thing can be more aptly classified as a concentration practice. The concentration practices I use include yoga, Qigong, mind games, and a breath control practice I've dubbed *Box Breathing*.

Box Breathing is named after its box-like ratio of inhale, retention, exhale, and suspension. This is my secret weapon in times of stress. It's simple, safe, and effective at creating a balanced, energized state, and a calm, focused mind. As of this writing, breath control for mental development is not taught in the West beyond a very small group of authentic Yoga professionals. One of my mentors, Gary Kraftsow, founder of the American Viniyoga Institute, is one such professional. Though I had been doing some form of breath control since my days of swimming competitively, sitting on the Zen bench, and during dive missions with the SEALs, it was Gary who taught me the science behind it. And he taught me how to integrate breath work into yoga and, by extension, any physical training program. Controlling the breath calms our thoughts, slows our heart rate, and regulates our autonomous nervous system. The mind is what compounds problems in times of stress. If we can control our mental response to stress, discomfort, or pain, then our physical ability to stay in the game and lead our team to victory is greatly enhanced. Box Breathing is our answer.

We've already looked at how to maintain positive focus using breath awareness to still the mind. Focus and concentration are closely related, though the mechanics are slightly different. A mind stilled through meditation has different qualities than an unfettered, focused mind able to zero in on a solution and pounce. Both mental states are important for the warrior and leader. When we begin a concentration practice, our goal is to be able to sustain focus on one thing without distraction. Breathing properly slows everything down so that you can concentrate on a fixed point for a longer period of time. This is what reduces stress and increases your sense of internal control. You now have the power to direct your mind where you please (focus) and leave worries, fears, and other threats outside this narrow scope of your sustained attention (concentration).

The yogis say that with enough deep concentration, one can know the nature of all things, all wisdom. We'll take a closer look at the benefits of expanding your awareness in Chapter Six. For now, let's settle for the practical benefits of controlled breathing and improved concentration, such as:

- Improve your overall health and sense of well-being- long term practitioner's sleep better, eat less, and have more energy
- Enhance longevity
- Heal from diseases such as cancer — when combined with belief, a positive attitude, and visualization
- Increase your cognitive intelligence
- Develop emotional awareness
- Enhance your mental and emotional control
- Remain unfazed and undistracted in the face of stress or a crisis
- Be a more persistent and creative problem solver
- Finish everything you decide is important to start
- Solve interpersonal conflicts
- Experience higher self-esteem, respect, compassion, and love
- Gain more insight and self-knowledge
- Be more present and attentive
- Develop contentedness and non-attachment
- Develop intuition
- Develop spiritual insight

This type of inner training requires daily effort. The good news is you can do enjoyable things to deepen concentration, such as the simple technique of Box Breathing, select yoga poses and sequences, and even reading. Further, the better you get, the easier it is to "practice" concentration at will, such as during physical training sessions or when playing a sport.

This skill isn't just for the Unbeatable Mind student or athlete who pushes the envelope physically. This practice will enhance performance in the boardroom, during surgery, while presenting a keynote. The level of control over your physiology and psychology to which I'm referring must be practiced and habituated until it becomes a routine skill.

BREATH CONTROL BASIC TRAINING

Breath control is the most important component to forge mental toughness.

To begin our basic training, it's important to understand that proper breathing works on three levels in our bodies. First, it enhances our lung capacity and breathing musculature, strengthening the immune system and regulating our neuroendocrine system. Second, it charges and balances our *energetic body* into a state of invigorated health. Yes, I'm referring to our energy channels (*nadis*) and their epicenters (*chakras*). The energy body is elaborate and has been mapped in great detail by quantum physicists and Buddhists alike (though it's mostly out of reach of Western scientific instruments at this time). Third, as discussed, proper breathing clarifies and focuses the mind.

During drown-proof training at BUD/S, trainees often drop because they have difficulty controlling the stress and fear caused by this simulated event. With hands and feet tied, they panic and flail, throwing their energy down the drain. However, those who have learned to control their breathing sail through the evolution. Let's look at the details of basic breath training.

When you were a baby, you knew how to breathe. For some unknown reason, most of us lose this knowledge with age. The average person takes fourteen to fifteen breaths per minute and uses a paltry one-third of their lung capacity. This leads to increased blood pressure, carbon dioxide buildup, and it fuels your monkey mind. The trained warrior will take three to five breaths per minute, greatly reducing the amount of carbon dioxide in their system while maintaining a calm body and mind.

There are three problems with rapid, shallow breathing:

1. You're wasting precious energy on all the extra breaths.
2. You're not bringing in the optimal supply of oxygen and life-force in each breath, leaving energy on the table and, consequently, shortening your lifespan.
3. You're not expunging all the stale air from the depths of your lungs. This habit incurs sluggishness, toxicity, and long-term health problems.

Learning to breathe correctly is imperative for optimal health. Let's get you back on track with this three-part relaxation breath technique.

Inhale deeply through the nose, filling the belly up with your breath like a balloon. On the exhale, expel all the air out through your nose. Draw the navel back toward your spine to make sure the belly is empty of air. Repeat this for three to five cycles.

Now, on the next inhale, fill the belly up with air but, when the belly is "full," draw in more breath with your diaphragm into the ribcage, causing the ribs to widen. On the exhale, let the air go first from the ribcage and then from the belly, drawing the naval back toward the spine. Stay with this for three to five cycles.

Finally, fill up the belly and ribcage and then draw in even more air into the upper chest, all the way up to the collarbone. You will note your upper chest rising and expanding. On the exhale, let the breath go first from the upper chest, then from the ribcage, and then from the belly. You will feel a relaxing, settling feeling as you release the pressure. This three-part breath exercise retrains you to breathe naturally.

Please note that the inhale and exhale are done solely through the nose in a slow and controlled manner. In fact, unless you're smoked in a workout and gasping for air, the nose is the organ for breathing. It warms (or cools) and cleanses the air of unwanted elements, such as dust, on the inhale. And nose breathing stimulates the nerves that activate the parasympathetic nervous system (especially on the exhale), countering the fear response of the sympathetic nervous system.

BOX BREATHING

Now that you know how to breathe, let's turn to my favorite training tool, which develops the relaxation breath and the skill of concentration simultaneously. I named it Box Breathing in 2007 when I introduced the technique because the pattern of the breath is a 1:1:1:1 ratio, shaped like a box.

Let's start by exhaling all the air from the lungs.

1. Inhale to a count of five (into your belly).
2. Retain and hold the breath to a count of five. (Don't clamp down and create back-pressure with this hold but continue the upward rise of the chest.)
3. Exhale the air slowly to a count of five (pushing the naval into the spine).
4. Suspend and hold the exhaled breath to a count of five.

That's Box Breathing.

If you feel dizzy or out of breath, use a three- or four-count technique to start. You can build up to the five-count method.

For a more profound impact with your training, add a powerful jingle or mantra on each hold, such as, "Getting better and better, stronger and unfettered." Choose a mantra that's five seconds in length.

Practicing Box Breathing at least once a day for five to ten minutes is enough—though I enjoy longer sessions of twenty minutes a few times a week. The technique can be used in short one- to three-minute "spot drills" several times a day, too, or before an important meeting or event. This is an omnipotent approach to check in and feed the courage wolf while managing your stress. Also—three for the price of one—this exercise strengthens your mental power and improves lung capacity. Box Breathing is so transformative that, with consistent execution, it will profoundly change your life.

BOX BREATHING

5 X 5 X 5 X 5

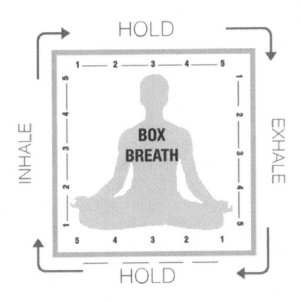

REPEAT MINIMUM 5 TIMES,
OR LONGER AS TIME ALLOWS

We've covered my three top secrets to mental toughness: understanding the power of choice, the vital importance of mastering concentration, and the transformational power of breathwork through my personal technique of Box Breathing.

Let's practice what we've learned.

We're going to start with a quick journaling exercise called Positive Fuel, and then move on to five or ten minutes of Box Breathing.

Exercise 4: Positive Fuel

Consider what kind of common negative fear loops may be present in your mind throughout your day. Acknowledge them here:

1.
2.
3.

Now commit to at least three positive mantras that resonate with you to interdict and replace these negative fear loops when they arise. Feel free to borrow from my examples: "Easy day." "We got this." "Piece of cake." "Looking good, feeling good, oughta be in Hollywood." "Every day in every way, better and better, hooyah, hey!" The point is to have positive fuel ready to deploy when negativity creeps in.

1.
2.
3.

Now, let's do the work.

Box Breathing

You can remain seated or stand if your knees or back are bothering you. If you'd like to incorporate one of your new five-second mantras during the intervals where you hold your breath, go ahead and choose one from your list — make sure it suits your *one thing*.

Let's begin. Inhale to a count of five, hold for five while counting or stating your mantra, exhale for five, hold for five while counting or stating your mantra. If you find yourself getting frustrated at this early stage in your Box Breathing practice, you may resort to Zen counting practice or the Fishbowl visualization technique. The point is to work on achieving concentration for a prolonged period five minutes or more is a good start. (You can also practice Box Breathing with one of my guided videos: https://www.youtube.com/watch?v=GZzhk9jEkkI.)

• • •

In the next chapter, we'll study the six powerful disciplines that come together to create self-mastery to develop self-esteem and be of service to others.

CHAPTER FIVE

SELF-MASTERY

"The outer conditions of a person's life will always be found to reflect their inner beliefs."

—James Allen

Before the SEALs, my career as a fledgling accountant at Coopers & Lybrand was driven by short-term goals of earning an MBA and CPA (showing a need for significance) and by long-term goals of financial independence (displaying a need for certainty). I was cruising along but didn't find the work very interesting or rewarding. Those six letters, "MBA-CPA," became my focus, and I wasn't going to quit no matter what. I was making great money in a prestigious job and had a career path shimmering out in front of me.

But my Zen meditative practices and warrior training were chipping at the outer shell of my ego, enough to allow my inner voice to be heard. *Mark, you're out of alignment with your purpose. Your passion is to be a leader, a warrior, and to find a grand adventure. Your principles are being compromised by chasing money, and your purpose is bigger than just being in business for the sake of a career.* I was growing more miserable by the day.

The greater the depth of my perceptions, the more disdain I felt for the greed and backstabbing behavior I was observing in the office — and I was a full participant in the charades. This collision of my worlds was disorienting. All the external indicators were green. I was getting all the right social feedback and the message from the home front was that I was kicking ass. (The Divines were a business family, period.) Internally, I had this brooding sensation that I was steaming away in the wrong direction.

After one of our Zen trainings, Kaicho Nakamura gave a lecture titled "One Day, One Life." He explained that a warrior experiences a lifetime in a single day. You see, the warrior doesn't take anything for granted. They live on the razor's edge of experience as if each day were their last. They avoid getting caught up in the dramas of life, steering clear of regrets and unnecessary desires by keeping things simple and practical. In order to experience one life in one day, the warrior trains his body, mind, and spirit to be at the ready.

I was moved by the lecture. For weeks, I thought about why the message resonated with me. It drove me to ask vital questions: What would I be like if my life had an all-encompassing purpose beyond making money and ascending the steps of a conventional career? How motivating it would be to wake up every day with that hair-on-fire passion to fulfill a deeply charged purpose.

This awakening allowed me to finally let go of the culturally sustained archetype about work and accept a whole new philosophy of life. To this day, I continue to train daily to uphold the standard set by Kaicho Nakamura's "One Day, One Life" speech. The discipline this concept represents is called self-mastery. It is developed by traveling the Five Mountains.

THE FIVE MOUNTAINS

Depending on your level of development and awareness, you will have different definitions of success. To me, success isn't about gaining control over your environment or focusing on external rewards like making a lot of money. Success in life is internal. It comes from developing mastery over yourself and using this skill to serve others in the fulfillment of your purpose. When this path is pursued, peace of mind is cultivated due to non-attachment to material possessions. Because you're in alignment with your purpose and your *one thing*, you always know your *why*. Your sense of well-being is balanced and strong. All your actions, decisions, and the quality of your relationships flow from this evolved, calm state of clarity. Attaining certain career milestones, by-products of true success, will happen, but we don't focus on these as goals.

When I finally found the courage to step out of the corporate game and join the SEALs, I discovered they had a similar approach to life. Both Seido Karate and the SEALs embody the philosophy that to actualize potential, we must take a balanced, "whole person" approach to training. If you're pursuing improvements strictly within the physical or the intellectual domains, other important aspects of your "self" will go undeveloped. You won't be living the "one day, one life" maxim, and miss invaluable opportunities to maximize your potential, meet your mission and serve others, and fulfill your purpose. The discipline of the warrior is to train for full-spectrum integration, ready to respond to any challenge with a virtuosity born of a clear heart and mind. In my experience, there are five primary domains of intelligence that must be developed for warrior-like focus and genuine success in life (as I've defined it above). This is what I call the Five Mountains of Self-Mastery:

1. The Physical Mountain: methodically developing the ability to control and use your body with all-around functionality. This builds confidence and self-esteem and makes you more useful in life and to your team. This includes the physical skills of strength, stamina, endurance, and durability. Honing these skills requires properly fueling the body, getting enough sleep, taking downtime to recover as needed, and learning to regulate the sympathetic and parasympathetic aspects of your autonomous nervous system.

2. The Mental Mountain: cultivating mental control and concentration and upgrading the content of your mind to ensure a positive contribution to the world. This includes learning to tap into your subconscious programming and rewire it as needed to master the skills — and acquire the knowledge — necessary to your personal or professional calling.

3. The Emotional Mountain: understanding, harnessing, and controlling your vast emotional power, developing self-esteem, confidence, and forging resiliency in the face of great challenges.

4. The Intuition Mountain: becoming an aware and intuitive leader by learning to look within and develop your sixth sense (to listen with your gut) and get Sheepdog Strong. (We'll talk about what it means to be "Sheepdog Strong" in Chapter Nine.)

5. The Kokoro Mountain: learning to lead and act with your heart, connecting authentically with others, and striving for an integrated consciousness that benefits all humankind. As mentioned in the Introduction, *kokoro* has Japanese origins and can also be described as merging one's heart and mind into action (acting from the whole mind), positive willpower, or a non-quitting spirit.

The Physical Mountain is covered in detail in my book, *8 Weeks to SEALFIT*, and beyond the scope of this work, but check it out if you feel compelled! Our focus is the other four mountains — training the intellectual, emotional, and spiritual aspects of your "whole person" in an integrated manner. This will set you on the path to mastering yourself at all levels and accelerate you toward higher plateaus of consciousness, where you will experience life at its fullest.

5 MOUNTAINS of SELF MASTERY

PHYISICAL

MENTAL

EMOTIONAL

INTUITION & AWARENESS

KOKORO SPIRIT

Accelerated Development as a Whole Person

THE SIX DISCIPLINES OF THE WARRIOR

No maritime journey of importance is ever achieved without a sturdy ship, a sophisticated navigation system, and a disciplined captain and crew. As you set out to tackle your Five Mountains, you will need disciplines with this magnitude of value to guide your journey, especially through stormy waters, which we all endure.

Before we go further, let's define *discipline*. Discipline has several common definitions, but for our purposes, we'll use this one: *Training to ensure proper behavior: the practice or methods of teaching and learning behavior patterns.*

The idea is to literally be a "disciple" to something larger than yourself. In this context, you must be a disciple to each of the Five Mountains of Self-Mastery.

There are three disciplines to follow on the road to self-mastery. The first is simplicity.

SIMPLICITY

When I was in the corporate world, navigating the political and social scene, life was complicated, a cacophony of discordant and emotionally charged egos colliding. When I jettisoned that world and landed in the SEAL teams, life suddenly got very simple. My mission was clear: hunt and kill the bad guys and protect the life we had back home. Personal possessions often got in the way. In this new light of simplicity, they were discarded. Communications between teammates were kept spartan and authentic. Lives were on the line, eradicating the BS of social politics. My life collapsed into training and conducting missions around the world. The straightforward lifestyle of the warrior was liberating. I try to live by the same standard to this day.

Let's break this down to a practical level. In the context of everyday choices, simplicity can mean being content with your present situation. And, yes, I'm suggesting you conduct an overhaul of your definition of contentment. You can have peace of mind and still have the desire for a better future. It's when we become weighed down with dissatisfaction and negative emotions that we tend to complicate things. It doesn't help to beat yourself up about your current state of affairs. Besides, it's distracting. Where you are now is a necessary step in your evolution, so be content while executing a strategy for where you want to go. This will immediately simplify your life.

Embracing simplicity offers another potent and liberating opportunity. It allows you to unburden yourself from extraneous commitments, material possessions, and unsupportive relationships. These things clutter the mind. Lightening the load, lightens the spirit. This principle extends to practicing moderation in speech, food, drink, and other habits. Too much of a good thing turns it into a bad thing. The Greeks understood this discipline, so much so that it's one of two statements inscribed on the Temple of Apollo in Delphi: "Everything in moderation."

Sometimes, I allow things to clutter up in some areas of my life — my closet, office, car trunk, to get specific. Maybe you do the same. A periodic decluttering of these spaces is an excellent way to experience simplicity and reconnect with contentment. Begin with your most cluttered space. Clean it and maintain it quarterly. Decluttering will help you avoid accumulating unnecessary possessions. Keep things simple. Look around. Do you see anything you can get rid of? Always be asking yourself these two questions:

1. Do I really need this now?
2. Can I live without it?

This simplicity practice leads to less attachment to material things over time. Detachment is a powerful attitude closely related to contentment. You can't take your possessions with you, though many have died trying.

DEDICATION

The next discipline is dedication. If you are committed to self-mastery, you must be dedicated to your training. After I endured two years of continuous training to become a Navy SEAL, I was somewhat surprised to learn that my number one focus as a "Team Guy" was to train more and train harder. It never ended, and it has transformed my life in several ways. First, training was not optional. It was as essential as eating and sleeping. Second, training was too critical to be haphazard. Most people have a half-assed approach to physical training and wonder why they don't get very far. Training like that would be a disaster for any elite team. It must be planned and purposeful and approached with a "crawl-walk-run" methodology. This requires dedication.

One of a plethora of unreal experiences from my SEAL days stands out when I think about dedication or what it takes to master a skill.

It was my first predawn freefall jump in the thick blackness of a moonless night, while the roar of the rotor blades from the chopper pierced the sky's stillness. As I flew off the ramp into the darkness, the wind buffeted me like a rag doll. I arched my back and leveled out, as I felt my body accelerating away from the bird. I looked at the horizon and saw a streak of sunlight penetrating the night. I also saw my SEAL instructor, Mike Loo, watching me from above as he swooped in parallel to my position. I did a 360-degree turn to face Loo for his next set of instructions. If I hadn't been hurtling through the air at 120 miles per hour, you would have seen my jaw drop. Loo was standing feet to earth, dropping like a bullet, smiling at me calmly. Then, he flicked his fingers and did a 360-degree vertical flip, landing feet to earth again. Loo then tapped his altimeter, causing me to look at mine. *Four thousand feet above ground level...time to pull.* I yanked my rip cord, deploying my parachute. It waffled up and caught air with a pop, and then drifted to a safe landing.

That moment with my instructor was indelibly burned in my brain as a display of total control over body and mind. I had witnessed mastery. But, of course, Mike was just doing his job. His control in the air was astounding but it hadn't come naturally. Mike had mastered his emotions and physical reactions, as well as skills specific to high altitude jumps, during his training. The guy had more than 2,000 freefalls under his belt.

A note of caution: Dedication must be counterbalanced with humor and reality checks. And don't forget to let "real life" flow. Being serious 24/7 won't move you along faster—trust me. Finding a balance is more effective for the long haul, and more fun. Based on what you've seen in pop culture and in the movies, you might expect that Kaicho Nakamura and my SEAL brothers were a stern lot. Nothing is further from the truth. Though we were all dedicated and intensely serious about mastery, we shared a lot of lighthearted and hilarious moments. I have no doubt that Mike Loo was laughing inside as he stood on air while plummeting like a meteorite, nodding to me as if we were hanging out on a street corner.

Try not to take yourself too seriously, and keep in mind that the journey is more important than the destination, so you should relax and enjoy the ride.

AUTHENTICITY

The third discipline we want to explore is authenticity. This will evolve naturally as you focus on self-mastery, but it's also important to make it second nature. As discussed, living authentically begins with discovering what drives you — your 3Ps and your *one thing* — so you can serve others in alignment with your internal compass. It is in this mind-body-spirit alignment, where the heart and mind are connected, that your character radiates authenticity.

I probably don't need to stress how challenging this is in our busy lives, which are built on an economic model that separates and pits us against each other in subtle ways. However, the quality of your relationships going forward will largely be defined by this. A lack of authenticity leads to diminished trust, creating a less evolved transactional relationship between individuals, corporations, or nations, and little, if any, real understanding or connection. These agreements — often built on legal details — are doomed for conflict. An abundance of authenticity will lead to enhanced trust, fostering transformational relationships and an inclination to seek common ground, a win for all. These agreements are built on an integrated worldview and are upheld with a handshake. No doubt we are a ways from that ideal, but what would you prefer? I prefer dealing at an authentic trust level, whereby we each write our own script from a place of abundance and honor.

Now that we're clear on simplicity, dedication, and authenticity, let's move on. The disciplines we need to be of service to others are compassion, abundance, and generosity. But first, a story to set the stage.

"MURPH"

Medal of Honor recipient Lieutenant Michael Murphy was killed during a SEAL mission in the mountains of Afghanistan. The riveting story was told by his teammate, Marcus Luttrell, in the book *Lone Survivor*. Heroics aside, the behavior of the late Lieutenant Murphy is interesting to look at in the context of our discussion of disciplines. "Murph," as he was known, demonstrated compassion for his team during the failed operation. When his team was discovered by a shepherd and his son, Murph had to pit the military rules of engagement against the local threat of a Taliban response (decide whether to kill or release the unarmed locals to protect his team and mission). He let them go, leading to disastrous consequences, as the locals did, indeed, inform the Taliban.

It's easy to second-guess the judgment calls of others from the comfort of our living rooms. And many special operators believe he made the wrong decision. But, the fact that his world-centric level of consciousness led him to act out of compassion, not violence, is what I find intriguing. What's certain is that he died a hero and with a clear heart.

Another big lesson we can learn from Lieutenant Murphy is how he served his teammates. After being overrun by hundreds of Taliban, Murph and the team fought like lions. But the situation was grim, so he tried to call in help. Unfortunately, the radio did not work in the mountainous terrain, so he resorted to a satellite phone. To get an uplink to the satellite, he exposed himself to enemy fire, knowing full well he would not survive. According to Luttrell, there was no hesitation in Murphy's decision to make this sacrifice, no second thoughts about self-preservation. Murph stepped into the open to call for backup, and that was the end. He lost his life. But if he hadn't radioed for backup, Marcus Luttrell would not be around today to share the story.

There is much ado about service in the philanthropic and religious communities. The doing of good works in the name of service is a nice gesture. However, this is not "Murph-level" sacrifice. Oftentimes, individuals or companies do it to look good or because their competitors are doing it. Sometimes, a person will provide some service through their church and be a self-serving jerk at home. These actions aren't authentic. The type of service that Murph modeled involved putting your team (family) before yourself at all times. This discipline requires three supporting attitudes: compassion, generosity, and abundance.

COMPASSION

Compassion, evolving from self-respect, embodies the ability to assume the perspective of others, with all the glory and suffering of the human race present in some manner. In our society, compassion has often been viewed as a weak trait in men (though this tendency is slowly changing). Warrior traditions have treated compassion as a strength that extends even to the enemy, as Lt. Murphy, through his actions on the mountaintop, displayed this in Afghanistan. Authentic warriors are the last to choose the fight but the first to pick up the weapon when duty demands it. To master compassion for others, one must possess self-respect, which is cultivated by clearing the slate of self-judgment and regret.

ABUNDANCE

Abundance is a positive expression of a highly evolved consciousness that recognizes there is plenty to go around in this world. It is the exact opposite of scarcity. Often, it is the bite-sized things that betray a scarcity mentality. I almost lost a finger at a barbecue thanks to a guy who was transfixed on a juicy T-bone steak that I was about to fork from the grill. Out of nowhere, his knife came down hard between my middle and ring finger as he exclaimed, "Mine!" *Ouch.* That snapshot was all I needed to know that an obsessive mindset driven by a scarcity mentality saturated this individual's every action.

Let's take a look at the somewhat recent trend of "doomsday preppers," who view the world's rapid rate of change as a signal that things are about to collapse and get ugly. Now, you already know that I believe in being prepared. I believe in being aware of the warning signs life gives us, so we can be proactive, instead of waiting for a crisis to come to our doorstep. But what I'm advocating here is that you can be mindful of these objectives as you continue to practice an abundance attitude. Someone with an unbeatable mind looks at how quickly things are changing and shifts from saying, "The world's coming to an end!" to "Wow, it's going to be an exciting future — how can I upgrade my personal and team systems to keep pace with the opportunities on the horizon?"

When you have an abundance mindset, you see that there is more out there for everyone, including yourself. Seeing the world in this light makes service orientation a no-brainer. You're no longer cornered by the perception that you must grab what's yours or seize resources at the expense of others. This mentality is hard to find today but is a powerful change agent for your growth. If you're concerned about the future of the planet and its dwindling resources and have trouble being optimistic about it, I recommend the book aptly titled *Abundance* by Peter Diamandis. He paints a picture of the future based on paradigm-shifting breakthroughs in technology, and he believes a global shift in consciousness will transform the Earth and solve intractable environmental and social challenges — ones that technology and human arrogance created in the first place.

GENEROSITY

If an abundance attitude reflects your view of how the world is and works, then generosity is an abundance mindset that manifests in your behavior with others. It's a transaction related to your time, talents, energy, and resources. The universal law of generosity states that the more you share, the more you have in life. When you truly believe there's enough to go around, regardless of the situation, life stops being a zero-sum game. Generosity of time, unique talent, support, and love allows positive energy to flow from you like a river forever replenished by the wellspring of universal energy.

And generosity transcends mindset. It flows from your heart, with a genuine desire for others to have what you have, to experience the same abundance you experience. You don't seek to gain at the expense of others. Generosity can be developed by becoming aware of your daily impulses toward scarcity and actively redirecting those thoughts with everyday basics:

- Do you tip at least 20 percent?
- Do you smile at people you walk by?
- Do you allow someone else to have the biggest steak on the grill?
- Do you help someone without being asked?
- Would you step up for your family or teammates in a time of need?

The Golden Rule describes an attitude of generosity, a version of which exists in every spiritual tradition. "Do unto others as you would have them do unto you." This is the Christian version. The interesting aspect of this rule is that the return is greater than the investment. Keep in mind, the reciprocated generosity may come back at a later time or in another form, but it will come back in greater measure. On the other hand, if you're a stingy hoarder with your money or time, you'll dry up like Ebenezer Scrooge. Your energy will burn out as you become more brittle and inflexible in thought and body.

Unbeatable Mind training requires personal discipline and practice, as well as cultivating the character traits described above. Together, they form the basis for the meta-disciplines of self-mastery and service. They also develop the foundation for an ethical stand, which will pave the way for growth toward higher stages of consciousness and a more fulfilling life. I'd like to close this section with a question and an allegory.

WRITING YOUR OWN SCRIPT

Do you write your own scripts? Or are you, like I was in my pre-Seido Karate youth, reacting to a script written by someone else?

A reporter was writing a story about the achievements of this man, a twin, who clawed his way out of poverty and bad circumstances to achieve great success. "To what do you attribute your accomplishments?" the reporter asked. The man responded, "I had no choice, you see. My father was a horrible alcoholic and abused my brother and me. I knew that if I didn't work hard and seek a better life, I'd become just like him." Curious about the fate of the other twin, the reporter tracked him down. He was destitute, living on the streets. The reporter asked the same question. His response was, "I had no choice, you see. My father was a horrible alcoholic and abused my brother and me. I was doomed from the start and didn't stand a chance."

You have a *choice* to be in control of your life. No matter the circumstance, you choose your thoughts and how to focus them. How you use your mind, body, emotions, intuition, and connect with your spirit is a choice. Do you leave this to chance, letting the preconditioning of life write your script, or do you take control and write your own bestseller? The answer is clear.

By maintaining simplicity, dedication, and being true to yourself, you will navigate your ship with precision through every domain of intelligence — the Five Mountains — to develop warrior-like focus and experience contentment and success in life.

Exercise 5: Write Your Own Script

Take five minutes or more to practice Box Breathing (using a mantra if that's your preference). Or you can do the Fishbowl visualization technique or Zen counting practice.

Now, take out your journal and write your script — a few positive sentences that focus on the obstacles you've overcome to get to where you are today. To what do you attribute your accomplishments?

Once you've written the power statement that exemplifies your resiliency as a human, pick a discipline you're going to focus on strengthening over the next few weeks, be it simplicity, dedication, authenticity, compassion, abundance, or generosity. Write it down!

Now, work on it.

• • •

Congratulations, you've made it through Section 1 and learned how to breathe to still the mind and calm the body, and how to redirect your negative thoughts to starve your monkey mind and feed positivity — two of the Big Four skills of Mental Toughness.

You've also obtained a keen understanding of the disciplines of self-mastery and the importance of knowing your purpose so you can be of service to others and experience true happiness.

In Section 2, we'll delve deeper into how to develop our awareness and learn about the attitudes that create the foundation for a strong leader. And we'll continue to work with these tools — breath control and mental control — as we examine the transformational power of visualization and goal setting to forge an unbeatable mind.

CULTIVATE
EXCELLENCE

CHAPTER SIX

DEEP AWARENESS

"If you know the enemy and know yourself, you need not fear the result of a hundred battles. If you know yourself but not the enemy, for every victory gained you will also suffer a defeat. If you know neither the enemy nor yourself, you will succumb in every battle."

—Sun Tzu

So far, everything we've been talking about has been focused on your evolution as a human being and a leader. This circles back to the concept of self-examination. In Section 1, we learned how to start creating mental and emotional distance from our negative thoughts and reactions by connecting with our witness. We studied how to start eradicating the negative junk we see in that space and upgrading our thoughts, patterns, and responses with a disciplined approach to self-mastery. We also learned how being service oriented is a natural human urge, and how it supports our personal evolution, naturally emerging at higher stages of development.

Now I would like to explore how an advanced awareness is essential to your cycle of growth. The happiest and most successful people in the world are also those who are most aware of their internal and external environments. They are constantly scanning both for threats and opportunities to grow and lead. To make a change or institute an upgrade, awareness is the starting point. After you then do the work and make the change, you become aware of further opportunities for growth. This plane of awareness will now expand from your deepest self through to all three spheres of experience in your life.

THREE-SPHERE AWARENESS

The day after I left the active-duty Navy, I was surprised by the change in my mental state and sense of self. One day earlier I had been part of an elite team and a self-contained system within the SEALs, both of which had a profound influence on my thinking and behaviors. My team influenced my mental toughness, my sense of purpose, and my confidence. My teammates had gone to hell and back with me, and I trusted them with my life. I had forgotten that I would be hard-pressed to find that level of trust in the civilian world. The system of the Navy was rigid and clear: I knew how much I was to be paid, what to wear, where to go, and how to act every day. Then just like that— boom— it all changed. On the first day my obligations and interactions were outside and independent of the United States Navy, I was without my team, and was free of any definitive instructions as to what to wear, where to go and when, how to act, or what do to with my day. It was blank as a slate can be. I felt both liberated and, as odd as it may sound, strangely intimidated. Most of us have had to transition out of some form of rigid organizational structure because these structures—military, corporate, academic, and so on—have dominated the twentieth century, and continue to dominate today. Keenly developing the awareness and perspective of how we integrate with—and are changed by—the various teams and structures is what I mean by three sphere awareness.

3 Spheres

I SELF

Interior - Intention
Trustworthiness
Self-Mastery
Beauty & Art
3PS
Self Leadership

WE TEAM

Interior - Culture
Trust
Shared Risk & Experience
Team Mastery
Ethics

IT ORGANIZATION

Exterior - Collective
Structure
Systems
Rules / Roles
Society / Environment
Body / Skills / Strength

As you reflect on your own life, you can identify those moments where you went through a major change in a job, a career, or even transitioned from school into the workforce and suffered a similar experience. The big "aha" for me came when I studied the Integral Theory of American philosopher Ken Wilber. I began to understand how we live in three distinct spheres, each arising simultaneously and each impacting one another. They are the "I," "We," and "It" spheres, which I also refer to as the Self, Team, and Organization, in the context of the professional realm. These three are interdependent and have causal effects on each other. Change one, and all spheres are impacted.

The I sphere is the realm of your individual, subjective self. It is your consciousness, worldview, beliefs, and desires. It includes your sense of what is right, wrong, beautiful, and ugly, and every one of us is utterly unique in our I spheres. Indeed, we are intimately concerned with this sphere. It is the realm of internal awareness; when we say we are working toward mastery, it is primarily in the I sphere that we do our internal work and register the results. This is especially important because it is here that we develop trustworthiness and authenticity in relationships. These qualities become increasingly impactful as we engage in the We or It spheres.

The We sphere is your inter-subjective space between two or more people sharing experiences and trying to uncover common meaning. This sphere can also be thought of as the culture of a team, community, or society. "We" is experienced within a family, a work team, or a tribe of like-minded people. It is in the We sphere that ethical codes of conduct, your stand, communications strategies, and leadership authenticity are expressed, and further developed. It is within this sphere that separation, racial bias and judgment arise based upon the disparate developmental plateaus found amongst others (more on this in Chapter Ten). If you have wondered why there is so much conflict in the world, then you can look at the intersection of I and We at vastly different stages of human development to find the answer.

Because we engage the We sphere, interacting with other people, this level involves both our internal and external awareness. It is with awareness of this sphere that the warrior scans the team or tribe, seeking to understand their perspective, as well as searching for threats and opportunities, spotting the mines on the minefield long before others do. Whether it's an unruly drunk at a restaurant that might accidentally injure you or your family, or an investor who seems interested in your new business venture, awareness in the We sphere helps you respond quickly, effectively, and successfully.

But the I and We spheres don't exist in a structureless vacuum of anarchy. Both are influenced and restricted by systems, rules, roles, and behavioral aspects of an organization and its members. These are referred to as the It, or organization sphere. This sphere includes the bureaucratic organization as well as the family system and its behaviors, or the team's org chart and the techno-economic system it's embedded in. As with the other spheres, the It sphere overlays the I and We. For instance, your job as a team leader is to remain aware of your team's actions and needs in the "We" sphere. Even as you remain aware of what you're bringing to the moment in your "I" sphere and how you are all working within the "it" sphere-structure of your mission and organization. It's about how you flow through these different aspects with heightened awareness throughout the day. You want to be aware of how you are interacting with the spheres in terms of your roles and expectations, your accountability and responsibilities, and even whether the roles of the organization and standard operating procedures of the system at hand are structured properly to serve you and the team.

As a leader, you are always poking around and thinking, "You know, we could use a system for that" or "That system is broken, and we need to rebuild it." The internal awareness of the I sphere, the sense of responsibilities to the team in the We sphere, and the external awareness of the systems and structures in place in your business, military unit, academic or non-profit It sphere, allow you to take rapid and effective action, resolving problems and reflexively responding to opportunities as a leader.

This distinction of I, It, and We may seem obvious when we read about it. Right? But it is not readily apparent. This is because we are inside the bottle and cannot read the label. It can be a powerful mental model to understand what is going on with ourselves and others at any given point in time. To use these distinctions as a model, you will insert yourself in a central intersection of the three spheres and ask yourself what is right or wrong, working or out-of-order, in your own I, We, and It spheres. Another approach is to place a teammate into this cross-section and see how they fare with the same question. The model gives us insight into the nature of the individual and collective human experience, which helps us be better people and make better decisions. I believe that for Unbeatable Mind performance we need to win all three spheres. We do this by aligning for maximum results in all three spheres, simultaneously. Let me use an example of a physical altercation I almost experienced to make this point.

I was walking down a dark alley in Kuala Lumpur, Malaysia during my life in the SEALs. I suddenly found myself walking past three rugged locals who stopped what they were doing to size me up. Crap, I thought. What am I doing on this route? It was late, and the area had a reputation for crime, and I had just become a We. I knew that I needed to maintain my cool and project strength, not weakness. I committed to winning my I sphere by breathing deeply, feeding my courage dog, and envisioning myself as powerful and in control.

Then they approached, and one made a move toward me. I sidestepped him, turned, and confronted the others. "Big mistake — I have no money and am not afraid to fight you all — and I will win." I said those words while maintaining a calm state of mind and visualizing myself handily defeating them. They simply gave each other a look, turned, and walked in the opposite direction. They had decided that the We moment of an altercation was not worth injury to their individual I selves. Their rough and tough facade dissolved into the background.

A moment later, a police officer drove down the alley and gave me a glance that said, "Bad idea, American." Had I engaged in a fight — the We moment of conflict — then the

It sphere of the local legal system, as well as the cultural norms and rules of the US Navy – would have collided into my I sphere reality, making my life miserable even though I had not instigated the altercation. The key was that in this episode I won in all three spheres. These victories resulted from comprehension. I won in my mind (the I), I won against the criminal cultural possibility of violence and theft (the We) by avoiding being a victim of their capricious act, and I won the system (the It) by not breaking any rules or laws (perceived or real) which would have landed me in the black hole of a Malaysian jail cell. When you can align and win in all three spheres simultaneously, you will come out on top all the time.

Let me try another story. You meet a girl through an online dating site and agree to meet her at a bar. Your I spheres are excited about the prospects and the newness of the situation. Your We sphere interaction is going fine, until suddenly a beefy man comes up and starts giving your date a ration of shit. Critical information is deduced in this situation, with rapidly shifting opportunities and threats. Turns out he's a boyfriend she hasn't broken up with yet. Suddenly, your We sphere collides with this new character and the rules and norms shared between him and the soon-to-be ex-girlfriend, cause your I sphere to ratchet up to awareness level orange (which we will discuss shortly). The guy slaps your date, so you jump on him, and a barroom brawl ensures. The cops show up and, the next thing you know, you're in the back of a patrol car as the It sphere now has its way with you. You reflect that your I sphere is now neither excited about the prospects of the new female relationship nor fearful of the fight with her thug boyfriend but wondering how the heck you are going to get out of this mess!

How quickly things can change. But what if you had progressed into this whole evening ensuring that you would win in all three spheres? For example, what if your internal awareness had led you to come right out and ask your date if she was seeing anyone else? She may or may not have been honest about her not-quite-ex boyfriend, but perhaps her answer would have prompted you both to meet somewhere new (where she'd be unlikely to run into another wooer). And let's say you were in the restaurant and your radar was up and running. It's likely your awareness would pick up that a guy, physically betraying early signs of agitation, was checking you and your date out a little too closely. You might even catch him before he headed in your direction.

With your external awareness fully operational, a number of options would have been available that would have resulted in going home safely rather than to the police station: You could have pointed him out to her and asked her to go talk to him, avoiding the confrontation (or at least getting you out of the middle of it!). You could have suggested leaving immediately for another dinner spot. You could have chosen to end the date right then.

There's another way to think about the three spheres with regard to a situation like this, which we will call "winning the three fights." My friend, Tony Blauer, teaches an entire self-defense system based on this principle. The first fight is in your own mind, which is questioning whether you have the skills, the power, or otherwise the ability to enter into this fight and win. Second-guessing yourself and negative self-talk erode performance. So, we need to learn to win in the mind first. The second fight is the actual altercation itself. Developing fighting skills are important to win the fight, which typically also means that you will avoid it altogether or deflect the energy to defuse it. This is hard to do if you don't have the technical skills and haven't already won in your mind. The third fight is against the system as described in the scenario above. So, despite possessing the mental and physical skills to defend yourself and the girl against this thug, it is plausible that someone calls 911 and the cops haul you in after finding you standing over the guy with bloody fists. Even if you handily took the first and second fight, that third fight is in the loss column. With Unbeatable Mind awareness you will be able to diffuse a situation like this. Also, if it's necessary, you'll handle the escalation of force gracefully so that you come out of it as an innocent bystander who tried to help, not another perpetrator getting charged with assault and battery.

YOUR BACKGROUND OF OBVIOUSNESS

While with SEAL Team 3, I deployed to the Middle Eastern nation of Bahrain for an extended mission. One day I was walking on the naval base with a Bahraini officer when he reached over and grabbed my hand to hold it. It was an awkward moment made even more so because he made no move to release it. In fact, he kept holding it while we strolled the base for about forty-five minutes.

As a twenty-eight-year-old straight guy, a Navy SEAL with a strong dosage of testosterone streaming through me, every cell in my body was screaming in discomfort. To say this act required emotional control at that stage of my life was an understatement. I understood, though, that this was normal to him, part of his culture, and it was simply my own background belief that made it awkward.

Who deemed that holding hands with a man was wrong? In Bahrain, holding hands with another male is a show of friendship and loyalty. Do we expect our norms to be the norms of other cultures? No. They will have their own norms and beliefs that we may not understand. What is obvious to others we may be blind to, and vice versa. We are quick to judge, and for that reason Jesus admonishes us to "... first take the plank out of your own eye, and then you will see clearly to remove the speck from your brother's eye" (Matthew 7:5).

Here's the point: Though we may easily see the shortcomings of the beliefs and behaviors of others, we often remain ignorant of our own limitations, which are equal or worse. I call this blindness to the patterns and hidden beliefs that drive behavior our background of obviousness, or BOO. This BOO is largely a memory-induced phenomenon of your past-oriented self and deep-rooted belief systems. It includes things such as:

1. Hidden assumptions about your life based upon the family and place you were raised, which show up as relative rules and beliefs — such as thinking people should look or act a certain way in order to be what's considered normal or accepted.

2. A mind primed to think a certain way by the dominant myths, stories, and language of your society. For example, people who believe that their government or way of life is right, the best, and full

of value for others, while other groups are wrong, immoral, ignorant, or otherwise have less value. Even the entire functioning of all societies is built upon a story, to include the economic, political and business memes. Change the story, and the society will change along with it. An example of this is occurring before our eyes as the story of the industrial world's use of "unlimited natural resources" is clashing with a new story of environmental disasters and global warming. The old story is not holding up to reality for most people who are seeking new storylines to define the future.

3. An emotional body corrupted by negative emotions denied or transferred at an early age, such as people who suffer from insecurities and fears of abandonment brought on by absentee parents or caregivers who withheld affection.

4. An individual stuffed with overheated media noise and incessant TV and internet usage may believe that famous or wealthy people are smarter or better than them; or by concluding the world is imploding based on the histrionic babble of bad news (note that although bad news seems to break hour upon hour, made all the more grim by turbulent headlines and graphics as sensational as Times Square, statistically, per capita, we live in the safest and most abundant period in the known history of mankind).

I mentioned that these attributes lie deep in your subconscious mind and emotional body. But they surface in

111

your conscious mind where they show up as beliefs and patterned responses to the stimuli in your life. Your BOO can trip you up in so many ways that it is a major relief when you finally begin to root out flawed BOO, that shadowy part of ourselves that we drag around like a kettlebell. Understanding BOO will lead to more clarity and better decisions, helping to avoid future regret. But doing shadow work takes guts. Many well-intentioned people back off when confronted with their BOO. Why? Because it is scary and often painful to acknowledge weaknesses and flaws and then take them on. The bigger the shadow, the more overwhelming the obstacle to doing the work. These obstacles can come in four flavors:

1. Not having the tools or perhaps financial means to hire a therapist or attend training
2. An inability to muster the requisite motivation and energy for the task
3. Fear of failure from diminished reputation, loss of job, etc. (after all, you would have to admit you aren't perfect!); the sister obstacle to this is fear of success, which inevitably would disrupt one's comfortable status quo
4. Not having the courage to open up the hood and do the deep work or simply blaming someone else for your flaws

ALIGNING WITH UNIVERSAL LAWS

You can't hide from your own beliefs. What you believe in colors every thought you have and action you take and has a profound effect on who you become. Likes and dislikes, opinions of other people, career choices, and even the food you eat are all by-products of your beliefs. If your beliefs are working for you, then you should be hugely successful, peaceful, and content. It will all come naturally. If that sounds like a pipe dream, then perhaps your beliefs need to be challenged. In fact, when is the last time you examined and earnestly challenged the core beliefs you hold dear in your life? Typically, this only happens when we hit a wall, and everything clatters to a halt. You push the same cherished buttons on the control panel, but the machine continues to sputter and break down. It's within these moments you are most open to examining new beliefs.

Socrates made this comment long ago: "The unexamined life is not worth living." But what does it mean to examine a life? In particular, your life? I think it is clear that he meant to examine your core beliefs before a train wreck forces you to. Really, does it make sense to go through life with an air-tight assumption that all the ideas we have ingested are unassailable? This is a dead-end road to an unexamined life. Examining beliefs will lead to new levels of resolve because you find deeper meaning and clarity about the nature of existence itself.

Beliefs come in two primary forms, relative and universal. Relative beliefs, such as I believe America is the greatest nation on Earth or I believe I will be met by a bunch of virgins in heaven, are formed through human interaction and are relative (meaning they change) based upon the values, expectations, and center of gravity of the individual and society he or she is from. They include norms such as religious beliefs and ideas about things such as success, health, and morality. Relative beliefs, which are taken as law by the believers, are heavily influenced by families of origin and pop culture. The disparate, murky, and elastic nature of these beliefs, though, is what leads to such diversity of lived experience on our planet, for better or worse.

Universal laws form the basis for a set of beliefs that won't alter within or across cultures. Beliefs such as, "I believe in the importance of treating others as I'd like to be treated" or "I believe there is plenty for everyone in this world," are universally understood and exist outside of the realm of human selfishness. These beliefs are beyond discrimination or judgment of race, class, or creed. What is universally true for me is also universally true for you, regardless of the context in which we are raised. For example, no matter where you go in this world, if you treat people the way you'd like to be treated, you will get more positive results than if you treat them like dirt. It doesn't matter which deity told you this was a good idea — it's universally true. Most people are raised in a culture biased toward scarcity because it's been hardwired into modern economic systems, but the moment you choose to check outside of that, everything changes. It is universally true that if you see the world as abundant, that abundance becomes your reality.

Philosophers of all ages have noted that goodness comes from aligning with universal laws and internalizing these universal laws into beliefs, while the potential for weakness, even evil, comes from moral relativism. Moral relativists have endless arguments about whether good and evil are part of the human condition, leaving it a choice to move toward one or the other, or whether these aspects of reality exist independent of the human.

Our approach at Unbeatable Mind is assume the role of being our own scientists and test a theory out on ourselves. We observe the results then implement what works and then discard what doesn't. My personal experience has led me to believe that the world itself doesn't care much about me, but when I aligned my beliefs and actions with Universal Laws then my life experience improved dramatically. To actualize this kind of a result, an examination of original underlying beliefs is necessary to see which are relative and which universal. If a belief is relative, then I recommend you put it under the microscope and be prepared to upgrade or discard it. If it is universal, then ask whether you fully understand and appreciate its power. Also ask whether it is possible you hold a competing relative belief that cancels it out.

Here is an example of a canceling belief: You subscribe to a universal belief in abundance, that there is enough to go around and there is no reason to hoard or see scarcity — no need to butt into a line or steal someone's steak off the grill. However, you could simultaneously believe that you are not worthy of the abundance you dream of because you were born poor, lack the right opportunities, didn't go to the right college, or are stuck in a dead-end job. In this basic example, it is apparent that though you could believe in the concept of abundance, the relative belief and corresponding emotional state around your self-worth contradicts and cancels it out. Not a healthy situation.

The confluence of your beliefs, values, expectations, and level of consciousness forms a foundation for your overall belief in yourself as a person. This impacts your willpower and self-esteem. In other words, if you hang your hat on relative beliefs, then you are at risk of relying on weak or outdated perspectives, empty values, and perhaps even ego-driven expectations to prop up your willpower and your drive to get the job done, whatever it is. Television executives and their ad-buying sponsors will eagerly be at your service to help out. If your beliefs are grounded in universal laws, however, then your resolve and esteem will be strong because your universe now has your back! It all has to do with certainty—how certain are you that you're doing the right thing? How confident are you in your decisions? If you're using building blocks that are relative, your entire belief system is like a house of cards, ready to be toppled by a meager wisp of unexpected revelation. Build on a foundation of universal beliefs, and you're on sturdy ground that is unlikely to waver.

Let me give you another example: a lot of guys in the military are in the service because they believe that American methods of government, economic management, and social structures are the best in the world and it's our responsibility to spread these ideals and practices to others who need our support. This is a relative belief. What happens to these sorts is they get sent overseas to war and are exposed to other cultures that see things differently. Suddenly these guys are thinking, "You know what? These people don't really want to live the way we do. They don't want us here at all. We're not heroes to them." Their entire belief system is shattered, and suddenly they're uncertain about why they are out there risking their lives.

Now in some cases, this isn't entirely a bad thing. When your worldview shifts and you realize you've been living on a belief system that's not ringing true any longer, and you can positively integrate that into a new belief system, guess what we can call that? Growth. The problem is that during these shifts, you're uncertain, and all of a sudden everything gets cloudy. Your commitment to a task might start to slide because you can't connect to that "why" anymore. At best, this can be a serious setback. At worst, such as in a moment of crisis, this uncertainty may get you killed. The space between the old and new presents us a choice: to press boldly forward into the unknown, or to slink back into familiar territory.

Like many military guys, in my mid-twenties I believed that serving my country was important to our way of life by projecting force for global security while spreading democratic ideals in the world. Twenty years later, my experiences had caused me to find flaws in that relative belief. Not that I stopped being a fan of the United States or military service, but I realized that other cultures have values and ways of life that suit them, and that they may be better off if they did not adopt a western consumer economic model and our form of democracy. I saw that my earlier motivations were fueled by a relative belief in American exceptionalism. This served me well at the time, until I began to align more with the universal law of "do no harm unless in self-preservation" and a belief that individuals and cultures have a right to self-determination within certain internationally accepted human rights boundaries. I had to realign my "why" as a world-centric warrior committed to promoting the ideals outlined in this book. Ultimately, this new world-centric warrior consciousness nudged me to retire from the military and use my skills to serve through teaching and inspiring a new generation of warriors and leaders.

Bottom line: An entrenched belief in yourself and your mission will come from acting in alignment with universal truths. With this approach to living an examined life, you may accelerate your growth toward a multidimensional and integrated perspective, leaving absolutism and rigidity behind. Only then will you find uncommon resolve by your side to back you up on worthy pursuits.

Here are some universal laws to reflect upon. You will recognize many of these and you may be able to add others to the list:

1. The law of cause and effect: this law states that for every cause, there is an effect. It is also known in the East as karma. Study the Bhagavad Gita.

2. The law of abundance: this law states that the world has enough for everyone who chooses to see the world as abundant. Study Peter Diamandis' *Abundance*.

3. The law of winning in your mind first before taking the first action: this law says that you will achieve victory each and every time if you first see it, say it, and believe it in your mind. Study Sun Tzu's *The Art of War*.

4. The law of attraction: This law operates somewhat passively on your environment. It says that what you fix your mind on, you will attract into your life. Like attracts like. Study James Allen's *As a Man Thinketh*.

5. The law of receiving: that you receive in proportion to the value you deliver in life.

6. The Golden Rule: do unto others as you would have them do unto you. Study the New Testament.

7. The law of surrender: this law states that instead of pushing against the tide, surrender to it, and you will find enlightenment and peace. Study Lao Tzu's Tao *Te Ching*.

8. The law of forgiveness: this law says that if you forgive yourself and others, you will release negativity and find happiness. Study the life of Nelson Mandela.

9. The law of non-attachment: this law directs us to detach from material things, ideas, and ultimately to life itself for lasting contentment. Study the writings of the Dalai Lama.

10. The law of nonresistance: this law is similar to non-attachment, but it specifically applies to nonviolence. It states that you should never meet force with more force. This response never solves anything and, in most cases, it just makes things worse. Fighting violence with violence should be a last resort and only done in self-defense. Study the lives of Gandhi and Martin Luther King.

11. The law of focus: similar to the law of attraction, this complementary law is very active, stating that whatever you focus on with intensity and duration will come to pass. Study Napoleon Hill's book *Think and Grow Rich*.

Now let's turn our attention to the practical matter of how one goes about examining their beliefs to clear them up to align more closely with universal laws. I propose a self-awareness practice, which I provide a brief description of below. I leave it to you to investigate this and the others further and integrate what works for you into your training.

Exercise 6: Insight Meditation

Select an internal story to focus on for this next meditation. The awareness of the story can come from a comparison to how others view a situation, such as a political viewpoint or your relationship with money. Often, these and other relative beliefs are greatly influenced by our family of origin and root culture and, as such, we have a deep psychological and emotional attachment to them. Rather than just assuming you're right and the rest of us are off, meditate deeply on it from multiple perspectives. Allow your awareness to rest on what comes up, trying to penetrate into the object of your attention. As you sink deeper into the process, let go of actively thinking about it. Rather, just observe it and quietly take note of what comes up, which will be insights about your point of view and attachment to the belief systems of your past that may no longer serve you.

This process can reshape your entire perspective by taking the core, underlying thoughts and behaviors you have and transforming them into a new way of thinking.

Allow me to share a personal example with you. After getting mired in several bad business partnerships, I used this practice to gain insight on why I kept repeating the pattern. After a few weeks of insight meditation, I had the distinct revelation that I was overly trusting of those who came into my business organizational sphere. I had learned to trust my teammates with my life in the seals, which led to the mistaken judgment of giving business partners the same level of unconditional trust. I realized that in the private sector there were folks from all plateaus of consciousness with differing degrees of trustworthiness. So, though I was discouraged by this uncomfortable fact, I had to learn to verify business partners before trusting they had my back.

Start with five to ten minutes of Box Breathing.

Now select an internal story and move on to your insight meditation. I bullet pointed the reflective process to help you through the practice:

- Rather than just assuming you're right and the rest of us are off, meditate deeply on your story from multiple perspectives.
- Allow your awareness to rest on what comes up, trying to penetrate into the object of your attention.
- As you sink deeper into the process, continue to be an observer. You may find that attachment to the belief systems of your past may no longer serve you.
- Now, briefly write your old story in your journal, followed by your new broader view of the subject or situation.

• • •

In the next chapter, we will learn how to align our thoughts, words, and deeds in a truthful and honorable manner and discuss six basic virtues that we must train carefully until they become integrated into our character, a habitual part of how we interact with others. These virtues provide fodder for a lifetime of work on your path to self-mastery.

CHAPTER SEVEN

TRUST AND HUMILITY

"The ultimate value of life depends upon awareness and the power of contemplation rather than upon mere survival."

— Aristotle

"Q" was a talented and respected enlisted SEAL. He gave the appearance of being fit and skilled and possessing a strong character. To be a SEAL, one has to exhibit unusual character to begin with. However, Q's actions during a single operation proved to me how much character must be ingrained daily and constantly refined. If you let your guard down, you could expose yourself to lapses of judgment and character erosion, as Q did.

On one particularly dangerous ship-boarding mission, Q held a key position within the team. Halfway through the op, while under the hull of the ship, in the blackness of the underwater night, things began to spin out of control. In a few critical moments when we were transitioning from dive status to the surface, Q lost focus and struggled to complete his mission-critical task. This triggered a cascading failure to ripple down the diver line as our rigs plunged to the bottom of the bay. My platoon's senior enlisted diver was dragged to the bottom of the ocean, where he was trapped without oxygen. It could have ended in disaster, but fortunately he was as an exceptional diver who could hold his breath for over six minutes. He was also very cool in a crisis. The chief dissected the problem and was able to cut himself free and ascend after several nerve-racking moments for those of us on the surface. This underwater drama played out beyond our view because the dark rendered the situation imperceptible, but later on during the mission debrief and in some private conversations with Q, I put together a complete and disturbing picture.

What actually led to the breakdown with Q was not the obvious technical screw-up, but a less obvious failure of character. He had begun to use a recreational drug while off duty, rationalizing that what he did on his own time was his own business and what we didn't know couldn't hurt us. But for elite operators, the job and commitment to the team requires untarnished, 100-percent focus and mental clarity. Anything short of that puts everyone at risk in the intense and confusing places we operate, as it did in this situation. Lucky for Q and us all that things did not go worse.

In the high-risk environments SEALs operate in, character flaws are exposed fast. But in business or other domains in life, it may take longer for a flaw to have its inevitable negative blowback. I don't use the word "inevitable" lightly; you may get by for a period of time, long enough to see some success, before the results of a weak character begin to dismantle your efforts, but it will happen. To succeed at the highest levels as a leader, you must habituate the virtues of a warrior into your character for true character excellence. Then these virtues will ensure your destiny.

Virtues are the heart of one's value system, which can be somewhat subjective as we each must decide what we value and what value that thing or quality has relative to other things and qualities. Terms like "family values," for example, only have meaning in the context of the person talking about them — what they are referring to is what they find valuable with regard to families. Virtues, on the other hand, represent something more hard-cut and observable. We can all pretty much agree on what bravery or honesty looks like, even though our particular culture may place a unique form of currency on these virtues as compared to, say, faith or charity.

Virtues, like values, are nothing more than words — unless we choose to practice them and integrate them into our character in private and public. Portraying a virtue in public but betraying that same virtue in your private life means you might as well be acting in a movie. It's not real, and it's not the same as truly embodying the virtue. Unfortunately, public figures are often clueless about this principle. Greek philosophers were so adamant about character virtues that they believed they defined one's value as a citizen. Heraclitus said that "character is destiny," and Aristotle told us that "to enjoy the things we ought to enjoy…has the greatest bearing on excellence of character," and "no one who desires to become good will become good unless he does good things." As far as more recent history, Ralph Waldo Emerson advised that "character is higher than intellect," and Albert Schweitzer said that "example is not the main thing in life...it is the only thing!" These philosophers are in agreement that your actions define your character. It isn't what you think or say that is most important; it is the actions you take, especially when no one is looking. So the question is: Do you act with virtues of excellence? If so, then you don't need to finish this chapter. My feeling is that we can all work on the character aspect of ourselves as long as we live, so I hope you read on!

With our analysis it should be clear that these excellence virtues are skills that must be carefully selected and then trained into bedrock patterns. So, what virtues have the most power for us? I will offer you my top six excellence virtues, which will provide fodder for a lifetime of work on your path to character mastery.

TRUSTWORTHINESS

The first virtue that Q compromised that grim night under the hull of the ship, was trustworthiness. Trustworthiness is the glue that holds relationships and teams together. It is evidenced when an individual displays qualities in action deemed dependable by others, such as:

1. They are aligned in thought, word, and deed and thus display a predictable integrity in their actions.
2. They follow through on all commitments.
3. They are courageous and don't shirk from responsibilities or challenging assignments.
4. They don't run or hide during a crisis but rather step up to lead and help out.

5. They are competent enough to get the job done well and are unafraid to ask the right questions!

6. They are supportive of the team and delegate and trust them.

7. Stephen M.R. Covey, in his 2009 book, *The Speed of Trust*, offers a simple formula for how trust speeds transactions between individuals and organizations:

Increased Trust = Increased Speed and Decreased Cost
Decreased Trust = Decreased Speed and Increased Cost

Consider life pre-9/11 and the creation of the TSA bureaucracy. Before 9/11 we had a high level of trust in air travel as a society. Due to the severe and shocking breach of trust on 9/11 by the terrorists, the speed of air travel as a whole decreased by roughly an hour domestically and often more than two hours internationally. Your time and out-of-pocket costs have also gone up significantly to cover the expense of new procedures and equipment for enhanced security. You can apply this formula to any interaction between individuals, teams, organizations and markets and find that it holds true.

So, trustworthiness is a character trait that has real-world transactional implications beyond one's personal or business reputation. In Q's case the trust he breached due to his untrustworthy behavior almost killed a teammate and jeopardized a mission. In a business dealing, a breach of trust can cause a transaction to fail, can degrade one's reputation, and increase costs to all parties. Personal and team trustworthiness must be placed on the highest priority list, measured, and practiced. But how?

First, let's look at a few common myths about trust and then dispel them.

1. Trustworthiness is a soft skill only. Wrong. Trust is a combination of soft and hard skills.
2. Trustworthiness is developed slowly, over time. Wrong. It can be created and destroyed quickly. The key is to develop the habit of maintaining trustworthiness at all times, which takes discipline.
3. Trustworthiness is just solely about integrity. Wrong. Though integrity is critical for trust to develop between parties, it goes beyond integrity and speaks to one's entire character.
4. Once lost, trustworthiness is gone forever. Wrong. You can make amends, say you are sorry, and then rebuild trust.
5. In business, it is simply too risky to trust. Wrong. It is essential to have trust for optimal performance in business, as in all areas of life. If you are trustworthy and must deal with a party you know to be untrustworthy or that you simply don't know well (a pretty common scenario in business situations), then trust cannot exist. However, this doesn't mean you can't do business period. Simply transact business and verify results, let trust build, and remain aware. As I said, though, real progress is only made when both parties have a high level of trustworthiness.
6. Trustworthiness is only relevant to individuals and teams. Wrong. Organizations have a reputation

based upon the collective trustworthiness of each person in it. Their trustworthiness is displayed in how their customers, peers, and society treat them.

When it comes to developing trustworthiness, what behaviors can you work on to turn trustworthiness into a virtue? Here are some ideas:

1. Talk straight — avoid spins, lies, double talk, and flattery.
2. Demonstrate respect — you want and deserve respect, so begin by showing respect for others.
3. Create transparency — avoid withholding information and keeping secrets unless absolutely necessary to protect intellectual property or to prevent someone getting hurt.
4. Right wrongs quickly — we all screw up, so admit it, and repair things as fast as possible.
5. Show loyalty — don't take all the credit or sell others out. Don't gossip!
6. Deliver the results that you promise. Better yet, exceed them.
7. Earn your Trident every day — meaning strive to improve your trustworthiness every day.
8. Clarify expectations — ensure that the explicit and implicit tasks of your mission and those that you delegate are crystal clear.
9. Practice accountability — start with yourself, and then demand it of your team and organization. But the buck always stops with you.
10. Practice authentic listening.
11. Communicate with brutal honesty — use the brief (pre-action review of the plan) and debrief process

(post-action review of what happened) to keep communicating at all levels so you can always be learning and helping others learn.

12. Learn to trust others by delegating and giving more responsibility and then providing support when inevitable failures occur.

The key is to open up the dialogue about trustworthiness with your team and be willing to expose yourself to vulnerability and direct, honest feedback from them. You may be surprised at what you learn about yourself and your teammates, and the discussion alone will increase trust between you. Building trust by forging our own trustworthiness will allow loyalty to also rise with the tide.

LEADERSHIP

The words leadership and integrity often show up on the value lists of most individuals and organizations. But the list is where things often end. Leadership and integrity are relative until measured and framed with a positive ethos. In essence, "integrity" really just means that what you think, say, and do are in alignment, so it could be either positive or negative. In addition, leadership without positive integrity is manipulation. You would be hard-pressed to argue that Hitler didn't exhibit integrity in thought, word, and deed. However, his was a negative ego, ethnocentric-based integrity that caused his leadership to be mass manipulation and control of the German psyche. Leadership integrity was completely missing from this equation. The horrific result with Hitler was xenophobia, deep suspicion, war, and ethnic cleansing. My point is that integrity in leadership must be framed within a positive service attitude in order to build trust and loyalty and lead to honorable results.

Leadership expert Warren Bennis says that "leadership is doing the right thing, while management is doing things right." This is a clever saying and gets you thinking about the distinctions between leading and managing. Leading has typically been associated with creating a vision, crafting a mission and motivating a team to follow you to the end and back to accomplish it. Management, on the other hand, has been associated with the technical side of organizing the efforts of the individuals and teams within the structure of the organization. This is a pretty old-fashioned idea, I believe, as the bureaucratic model of organizing falls away into self-managing companies and integrally informed organizations. Ultimately what we are coming to is a need for leaders to be excellent self-managers and inspired leaders with integrity. We can simply look at this as leadership integrity, where the leader's thoughts, words and deeds are aligned in I, We, and It.

Aligning thoughts, words, and deeds in a truthful and honorable manner takes serious work, especially after learning how messed up our thinking can be. It requires courage and discipline to do the work, but this is super-critical. The decisions we are required to make are going to be even tougher in the future. Mistakes can lead to grave consequences: recall President Clinton's behavior in office. Mr. Clinton was a smart, pleasant, and remarkably effective politician. However, he was a horrible self-manager and lacked leadership integrity, as evidenced by his breaching the trust of his office and then lying about it. Here he was the President of the United States, an office that ideally, if not implicitly, requires a high degree of trustworthiness, honor and integrity, and he was sleeping with the interns and lying about it under oath. There was no integrity to be found between his thoughts, deeds, and actions. Moreover, there was no honor. He still couldn't take the "hard right action" even though he knew what the consequences could be. These gaping character defects are a sure sign that leadership integrity was absent. Though one may aspire to, and even attain, positions with tremendous power and influence, character excellence will remain beyond one's grasp without the virtue of leadership integrity.

A SEAL mentor of mine, Captain Jim O'Connell, used to say that a way to "gut check" for leadership integrity was to ask if you'd be thrilled to read about your pending action in the next edition of the New York Times. I find this to be a great guideline, one I am sure President Clinton wishes he had applied when contemplating his next action with Ms. Lewinski!

One time during a SEALFIT training, one of the students displayed a lack of personal leadership integrity when he did an about-face 10 feet before the turnaround point on a run. It was dark and he thought he was alone, but he was held accountable by a coach observing from the shadows. Cheating, especially on the small, seemingly inconsequential things, degrades integrity and chips away at trust. The short-term gain is soon demolished by the regret, shame, and degradation of respect that accompanies the inevitable exposure of the lie, not to mention the anxiety that envelops you while living in fear of exposure!

Good decision-making simply cannot occur under these conditions.

However, aligning thoughts, words, and actions in leadership integrity doesn't mean you have to always tell the truth or turn in a friend who slips up. There are situations where wisdom dictates a more sensitive response over a blanket policy of blurting out the truth to anyone within earshot. I was once contacted by a young lady looking for information about her SEAL dad's heroic exploits in Vietnam. The problem was that her dad was never a SEAL, rather he was posing as one. The news put me in a dilemma: Was it my job to expose this guy's fraud and protect the integrity of the SEAL name? My initial reaction was to do just that. But how would the girl's life change when she found out her father had been lying for her entire life? I wondered if it was my duty to be the judge, jury and executioner in this case? I decided the answer was no; I would not expose the man's fraud to her and dash their relationship; rather I would leave it to him to live with his dishonor. When I responded to her email, I simply said that the information she was seeking was not available to me.

If you've followed along closely, then you're well on your way to developing leadership integrity and acting with honor. In the Unbeatable Mind training we have a practice I call "authentic communication." This is a great tool to develop leadership integrity as it pertains to aligning your thoughts and words. The practice is to first pause with a breath before speaking, and then speak only if:

- What you have to say is true, as best as you can determine.
- And what you have to say is helpful or wise.
- And if what you have to say comes from a place of love and respect—meaning it's positive.

Then you will follow up your words with action to fulfill your commitments. When routinely habituated, this authentic communication tool will leave words of negativity and low value unspoken, and what is spoken will have increased power. Then the actions that follow will be anchored in truth, wisdom, and love as well. My guess is the world would also be better for the silence that would result if we all practiced this!

HUMILITY

Following and leading are two sides of the same coin; you can't have one without the other. Those who seek to lead without being willing to follow may gain some ego blast in the short run, but they typically fail in the long game. This attitude of serving through being a great follower is not a trick or tactic of leadership but rather another character trait that developed through the twin forces of experience and intent.

Taking your eyes off yourself and serving your teammates requires the humility to follow and support them most of the time. When the time or circumstances are appropriate for you to lead, you bolt out front and lead by example, with integrity and inspiration.

Thus, I feel the best way to cultivate character excellence and authentic leadership is not to leap in immediately to "earn your leadership stripes" (unless you have no choice) but to act with humility by watching carefully and being helpful as a follower. In the SEALs, officers are the leaders responsible for the mission, but at every phase there is usually someone else leading the charge — for instance one SEAL will lead the dive, another will lead the jump, a third will lead the direct-action raid, and so on. It is expected that the officers get out of the way and let these guys do what they do best. The officers who don't learn to trust their teammates, and to follow, usually don't fare well. In allowing subordinates to lead key parts of the mission, I'm giving them the opportunity to grow, to learn, to fail. And in reality, most of those SEALs, in those situations, had more skills and experience than I did in that arena. So yeah, I often found myself serving and supporting others to lead in my stead. I had to develop the humility to check my ego and say, "This is their turn. They're smarter at this or they're better at this or they've got the better idea or they're stronger." I had to recognize that there may be instances where I would be fatigued or injured, or for whatever reason just wouldn't be as equipped to make the right call. I had to learn to say, "You've got this, buddy, because you're going to do a better job than I am." You can't be good at everything, all the time. Knowing that is the kind of humility that earns trust and loyalty.

When I was a newly minted ensign in the SEALs, I knew I was supposed to lead, but it would have been my ego up on stage if I had tried to take control before I had any experience of what it really meant to operate in the field. So when I was recruited into my first platoon, I didn't set out to actively lead the men but rather to follow and learn from them, seeking to earn their trust. They knew I outranked them and that I would be held accountable if anything went wrong. But because of the way leadership is shared in the Teams, I also knew they would protect me in that event. This experience was a powerful lesson on humility: To lead you must first learn to follow. Again, humility reveals your true character excellence and earns you the trust you need to lead effectively.

If you're not in a leadership role, this virtue still comes into play. A good rule of thumb is to try to make the leader's job easier through your actions. You will gain the trust and respect of the team, and when needed, you will be called upon to lead. With this attitude, your time will soon come. If you force the issue, you can put yourself and the team at risk. Like with the SEALs, remember that within the fabric of a strong team every teammate has the capacity and character to lead. Everyone is simply awaiting the opportunity to serve in a leading role. You can also practice humility by sharing the credit for the team's successes, whether you were the one who had the big idea or were the one in charge.

RESPONSIBILITY

Responsibility has many levels and presents itself in many different forms. Warriors and spiritual leaders accept the highest form of responsibility: for the lives of others and the well-being of the human race. Corporate leaders are meant to accept responsibility for their organizations and teams, and we are all individually responsible for our thoughts and actions. An organization's transaction with a customer conveys with it the responsibility to fulfill their end of the bargain. You can see how being responsible has a big impact for the development of trustworthiness and loyalty. When you commit to your responsibilities as a virtue, then those who rely on you or whose success depends on you executing your part can rest a bit easier. They trust that you're going to carry your load, so they can commit fully to their part. In a strong team, responsibility means there's a sense that we've all got this together. Everyone has each other's back, and trust goes through the roof. As do the results. On the other hand, ignoring or abdicating responsibility breaches trust and erases loyalty lightning quick.

Accountability is the flip side of responsibility. When responsible for something or someone, you are held accountable for the consequences if things go wrong. Notice that there is no need for accountability when things go right. When things go wrong, however, is when your character goes on display. We observe a failure of courage in leaders when they don't accept full accountability when things go south. Images of political and business leaders denying involvement in scandals (such as Bill Clinton and later his wife, Hillary, with Benghazi) and pointing the finger far exceed reports of leaders accepting accountability. I am reminded of the CEO of British Petroleum, Tony Hayward, and his handling of the Deepwater Horizon oil spill in 2010. Hayward was cavalier and downplayed the risk to the environment and wildlife, even denying full accountability of his firm. He was like the teammate who, when the proverbial shit hit the fan, immediately shifted focus to cover his own ass. But in this case, Hayward was the CEO, so he was trying to cover not only his own ass, but the company's ass as well. The responsible thing to do would have been to step up and take ownership of the situation, to become a face for accountability and a positive force for solutions. Hayward could have gotten in front of the clean-up effort, taking care of the environment and the people who were adversely affected by the spill. Most people respond very positively to people who accept accountability with grace, even in a major disaster such as this one. Instead, Hayward's words and actions ultimately diminished trust among shareholders and the board, and his job came to a disgraced end.

Accountability extends to your teammates as well. One of the SEAL ethos statements is to "take responsibility for your own actions...and the actions of your teammates." This is a burden gladly accepted when you work with those you must trust with your life. However, when the risk is lower, as in most professions, that level of accountability is rare. Part of this is the fault of the systems that evolve with large organizations, as there is too often an emphasis on micromanaging and identifying who is responsible for failures in the sense of blame, rather than a focus on accountability and moving quickly to identify holes that need to be patched for next time, as in the SEAL debrief process. If each member of the team could make the mission and the team his responsibility without the restraint of excessive rules and regulations, and fear of being reprimanded (or worse) if things go wrong, and if each member could be held accountable to that standard of totally shared responsibility for the success of the team, you would have a powerful multiplier effect.

DETERMINATION

When I first set foot onto the fabled BUD/S training "grinder," I read the saying "The Only Easy Day Was Yesterday" (TOEDWY) written in gold on blue above the asphalt. It is a simple, yet profound statement that became my daily companion as my character was ground down and rebuilt over nine long months. Did the saying mean that yesterday was easy, or that today was going to be harder than yesterday? Nope. None of that really mattered. What it meant was that I had to deliver results with all I had — right here and right now. It meant I had to show up and put out 100 percent and then do it all again tomorrow. The memory of yesterday is easy because it is over, and tomorrow hasn't happened yet, so don't worry about it. Just focus on performing right now.

That saying was speaking to the need to develop determination, which goes hand in hand with the warrior-like discipline we've been talking about. TOEDWY encouraged us to remain determined to stay focused 100 percent, every individual moment, to keep driving forward. It encouraged us to learn new skills, gain new knowledge and to perform under duress and in all sorts of crazy situations. Those who accomplished this every day for the nine months (and beyond) had the privilege of serving alongside America's finest warriors.

PERSEVERANCE

If determination is the will to keep showing up and putting out 100 percent every day, then perseverance is the discipline to follow through and keep on going no matter what obstacles stand in your way.

During Operation Desert Storm a SEAL buddy of mine, Lieutenant Dietz, ran a highly successful diversion mission that tricked Saddam Hussein's forces into believing the US Marines were storming their beach. It was a classic "frogman" operation, but during the planning they struggled with how to move huge amounts of explosive to shore. Bringing the C-4 in by boat would increase the risk of detection. Swimming it in would make the loads smaller, but it was still problematic because it would require multiple trips back and forth and, in the interim, would expose the team to sharks and, if spotted from shore, vulnerable to attack.

Finally, a younger SEAL suggested floating in the C-4 haversacks on boogie boards. After a few moments of disbelief, Tom decided he liked the idea and sent a request for blacked-out boogie boards to the headquarters in Coronado, California. The desk-bound combat vet who received the request said out loud: "What the hell? I thought we were fighting a war over there!" Once the operational nature of the request was understood, however, the boards were sent, the trick worked, and the mission was a success.

There are a couple of points to this story: First, SEALs will always persevere to "find a way or make one." Second, they will never give up. SEALs persevere against all odds because they believe that failure is not an option. This doesn't mean that they can't fail or that things never go wrong; rather it means that they don't accept the concept of failure. You don't fail, you find a way, make a way, or learn again how not to do something. Learning what doesn't work and creating a new way is a success. With this approach to learning and mission execution, you can't fail in the traditional sense of the word. You simply keep trying until you succeed, learning through trial and error along the way. That's the virtue of perseverance at work.

To become as innovative and persistent as a SEAL requires a higher degree of risk tolerance and commitment to the task. It must start with your self-dialogue. As Yoda implores: "Do or do not. There is no try." Never suggest something can't be done, and if you decide to do something, then commit to seeing it through. Learn to adapt, improvise, and overcome any obstacles as you find a way or make one.

Now all of this sounds simple, right? But for SEAL-style perseverance to be realistic, you must ensure from the beginning that your goals are SMART-FITS targets. We'll dive more deeply into setting up your win from the start with proper target selection and goal setting in Chapter Eight, but for now, learn to apply these selection criteria and you will find that perseverance naturally becomes a part of your character:

1. Be optimistic and expect to win.
2. Make sure that the goal is very motivating to you and your team.
3. Burn with desire to win or achieve the goal. Ask yourself how badly you want the victory before you decide to act.
4. Understand the delta (difference) between your skills and knowledge now and what will be required to succeed at a high level. If the delta is

too much to overcome in the time frame you have, then you should wave off and choose another mission.

5. Ensure that you have the mental and physical capital to pull it off in a way that does not impact other mission-critical goals.

6. Once you commit, then burn your boats, press forward, and never, ever quit!

• • •

As you embark on cultivating your own personal virtues for excellence, it will be inspiring to read the Navy SEAL ethos. The ethos (and shorter code) is a great set of values to model in your own life. The SEALs take great pains to habituate these values through rigorous daily training as well as the example of the warriors through each successive generation. Here it is:

The Navy SEAL Ethos

In times of war or uncertainty there is a special breed of warrior ready to answer our Nation's call. Common citizens with uncommon desire to succeed. Forged by adversity, they stand alongside America's finest special operations forces to serve their country, the American people, and protect their way of life. I am that warrior.

My Trident is a symbol of honor and heritage. Bestowed upon me by the heroes that have gone before, it embodies the trust of those I have sworn to protect. By wearing the Trident I accept the responsibility of my chosen profession and way of life. It is a privilege that I must earn every day. My loyalty to Country and Team is beyond reproach. I humbly serve as a guardian to my fellow Americans always ready to defend those who are unable to defend themselves. I do not advertise the nature of my work, nor seek recognition for my actions. I voluntarily accept the inherent hazards of my profession, placing the welfare and security of others before my own.

I serve with honor on and off the battlefield. The ability to control my emotions and my actions, regardless of circumstance, sets me apart from others. Uncompromising integrity is my standard. My character and honor are steadfast. My word is my bond.

We expect to lead and be led. In the absence of orders I will take charge, lead my teammates and accomplish the mission. I lead by example in all situations.

I will never quit. I persevere and thrive on adversity. My Nation expects me to be physically harder and mentally stronger than my enemies. If knocked down, I will get back up, every time. I will draw on every remaining ounce of strength to protect my teammates and to accomplish our mission. I am never out of the fight.

We demand discipline. We expect innovation. The lives of my teammates and the success of our mission depend on me — my technical skill, tactical proficiency, and attention to detail. My training is never complete.

We train for war and fight to win. I stand ready to bring the full spectrum of combat power to bear in order to achieve my mission and the goals established by my country. The execution of my duties will be swift and violent when required yet guided by the very principles that I serve to defend.

Brave SEALs have fought and died building the proud tradition and feared reputation that I am bound to uphold. In the worst of conditions, the legacy of my teammates steadies my resolve and silently guides my every deed. I will not fail.

The SEAL Code (Short Version of the Ethos)

- Loyalty to country, team, and teammate
- Serve with honor and integrity on and off the battlefield
- Be ready to lead, ready to follow, and never quit!
- Take responsibility for your actions and the actions of your teammates
- Excel as warriors through discipline and innovation
- Train for war, fight to win, and defeat our nation's enemies
- Earn your Trident every day

Exercise 7: Contemplation

Contemplation is similar to insight meditation but, instead of internally reflecting on a belief or behavior that's been cultivated by your environment, you will choose external source material that compels you, such as one of the study materials mentioned in Chapter Six. This can also be a book or documentary or a podcast you've listened to but never invested a lot of thinking time into. You can also choose one of the six virtues I've defined in this chapter or one of their complementary stories. That might feel like the most reasonable way to practice a contemplative meditation for the first time — by keeping the source material brief and straightforward.

Open yourself to the new ideas and principles in the material you've chosen. Then, compare and contrast your personal actions, integrity, and standards with the object of your contemplation. Reflect on how you can move in the direction suggested or the direction that your witness knows is best. This can be very motivating and lead to a strong desire to grow toward the ideal presented in the external source material.

Let's start with five or ten minutes of Box Breathing.

Then, move on to the contemplation meditation.

On completion, take out your journal and briefly write about how reflecting on the source material opened your mind to a new and broader viewpoint. And write about what it taught you about yourself.

Great work!

• • •

In the next chapter, we will learn about the top mental models the seals use for decision-making and goal setting. You will also learn that the best way to reach a goal is to be realistic, learn to prioritize, and be prepared to fail forward fast.

CHAPTER EIGHT

FAIL FORWARD FAST

"A goal is a dream with a deadline."

— Napoleon Hill

It is clear now that erroneous thinking is common and leads to botched communications and mission failure all the time. The mental roadblocks we encounter in attempting to manage our brain zoo produce four productivity killers:

1. **Procrastination**: delaying action due to imperfect information
2. **Perfectionism**: delaying action due to an imperfect plan
3. **Analysis paralysis**: delaying action by trying to analyze too much information
4. **Groupthink**: taking the most tepid action poisoned by the confirmation bias of the group

Using mental models will reduce the frequency with which we have to deal with these killers and, with enough practice, squash them altogether. Mental models frame a problem with simple questions and create a standard for how to make a decision or create a plan. Indecisiveness and an inability to act is what creates issues like procrastination and paralysis analysis in the first place.

In the SEALs, we used a number of mental models with great success. In Book 1 of the *Unbeatable Mind* Series, we will discuss SMART-FITS goal setting and my *fail forward fast* philosophy, using the OODA Loop. To kick off the discussion, let's review the primary principle underlying all mental models: KISS!

KISS PLANNING

When I planned my first mission in the SEALs, I used a flip chart easel and the ancient industrial-engineering art of flow charting. The diagram was crowded with boxes and arrows depicting the entire mission, from planning stage to post-mission debrief. It was a cumbersome process to say the least. But when it came down to briefing the guys, the KISS rule prevailed, and the chart was tossed and the operators simply asked questions and talked their way through the mission. We visualized everything that would go right and anything that could go wrong beforehand. Then, we stepped outside, boarded the helo, and just did it. The only thing that has changed since those days is the tools we use.

The flip chart has been replaced by a suite of mission planning software, a projector, and a bevy of laptops, but the KISS rule still applies. At its most basic level, it means that we must focus on the most uncomplicated means to execute a plan. Too many moving parts can lead to confusion and gridlock in a crisis. All KISS plans need to be created using a mental model to ensure success.

SMARTP-FITS GOALS

It is no stunning news flash that properly selected goals, tied to your *one thing* and executed with a KISS good-enough plan, will propel you toward mission accomplishment. Goals not tethered to your purpose are wild goose chases, and a purpose without SMARTP-FITS goals is a fantasy awaiting regret. Unfortunately, most of us aren't aware of this tactic at an early enough age to allow for massive success. This seems so fundamental that it's astounding to me that mental models for goal setting aren't taught in grade school. Perhaps most teachers don't know how to do it? We are left to figure it out on our own by joining an elite military unit or cracking a book like this one. The most successful people are those who employ the principles in this chapter well. This skill is so crucial that it holds a place in the Big Four of Mental Toughness taught to the SEALs. This is Goal Setting.

It is important to note that goals can either be "being" goals or "doing" goals. In other words, goals help us "do" things (accomplish tasks) or "be" someone (reach an achievement). Both are important. Being goals are typically long term and centered around your development, such as mastering the Unbeatable Mind tools and practices or gaining specific qualities such as being a deeply connected world-centric leader. Doing goals are often lumped into a subset of a being goal, such as gaining a specific skill or reaching a milestone required for development or your overall mission. For instance, if a being goal is to become an elite warrior serving America, then a doing goal would be to earn the Navy SEAL Trident. And, to earn that trident, you would have had to achieve another doing goal of maximizing your scores on the initial entry tests to earn a contract to attend BUD/S.

The first order of business when selecting a goal is to consider whether it's right for you in the first place. Is it aligned with your purpose, vision, and mission? Goals that align with these will build the foundation of your future success.

FITS Targeting

Let's start by ensuring your goals or targets are the right ones. Do they fit your skillset? Are they important enough to engage in compared to other goals? Is it the right time for this goal? Is it a simple enough goal to execute in linked increments?

I came up with the FITS tool to rule out any unreasonable notions your monkey mind might conjure up. The FITS formula ensures a goal suits you in terms of your skill level and ability to commit, and it's in alignment with your greater purpose.

Fit: Does your goal fit you and your team in terms of your skills, resources, time, and personality? Is it reasonable or a long shot? Will the return on your investment in time, resources, and energy be worth it for this goal, or should you be looking at a different goal with higher return on investment?

Importance: Is this goal strategically important to achieve your mission or purpose? Will your mission fail if you do not achieve this goal? Is there another more vital goal you should be directing your precious energy toward? **Timing**: Is this the right time for this goal? What has to happen first for this goal to become a realistic achievement? Is there some other goal or target whose timing trumps this one? **Simplicity**: Is this a KISS goal? Can you break the goal into smaller micro-goals, *aka* steppingstones, to increase its simplicity and gain momentum toward actualizing your vision?

F.I.T.S

FIT - IMPORTANCE - TIMING - SIMPLICITY

Target Selection Tool

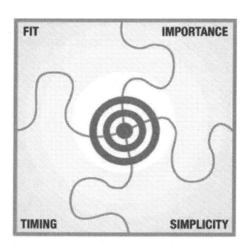

All four pieces of the puzzle must fit
for it to be an ideal target.

Once you are certain that your target or goal FITS you (and your team if applicable), then move to step two and positively state it in SMARTP terms to maximize your chances of success.

SMARTP-FITS goals are specific and detailed. They are measurable, progress is easily calibrated, and they are assessed as achievable. (Achievability speaks to your skills and available resources.) Goals that are aligned with your purpose and set with SMARTP-FITS rules back each other up like building blocks — they set the foundation for your future.

A few years back, I set a goal to improve a physical skill for the CrossFit Games. I declared that I would learn to do double unders effectively in three months. (Two revolutions of a jump rope in a single jump is a double under.) Two months later, I hadn't gotten close. This is when I realized that I had violated my SMARTP-FITS goal-setting method. So, I asked myself: "Mark, why take on any goal unless you intend to take it seriously?" And, I revised.

I will consistently perform twenty double unders in a row by March thirty-first. This was my SMARTP statement, which worked because the goal was:

- Specifically stated
- Measurable (twenty)
- Achievable (I could do about five in a row)
- Relevant (I wanted to compete in the CrossFit Games Open)
- Time bound (I gave myself a doable, thirty-day deadline)
- Positively stated

Plus, I had already determined that the goal Fit me, was Important to my immediate

future — meaning, the Timing was perfect — and it could be Simply achieved, as I owned a rope and could practice anywhere. And I'm always Postive-focused in stating my goals. That's a no-brainer. I wrote the goal down and checked in weekly. Do you think I hit it? Easy day.... But if I hadn't restated it in those terms and given it proper attention and consistent energy, I'd still be wishing I could do those damn double unders.

Let me dig deeper into why the SMARTP-FITS decision tools work so well. First off, properly selected targets help guarantee you're focused on the right things, while well-articulated goals ensure you're employing radical focus and determination. Without refined targets connected to your purpose and mission, you can get distracted or lose energy in the process. Properly crafted goals replace fantasy with reality and mobilize efforts with a deeper level of commitment. No more wandering or stumbling with your personal and professional initiatives.

My friend, Kyle Maynard, set a goal to climb Mount Kilimanjaro, a lofty goal by anyone's standards, but attainable, as many have climbed that mountain over the years. Here was the hitch: Kyle doesn't have any arms or legs. Most people would consider his goal inconceivable. Were it not for his incredible determination, it would have been. He'd made a promise to a dying friend to spread the man's ashes at the top of the mountain. And so, fueled by a powerful *why*, Kyle took more than two years to plan his adventure. Though others may not have understood, the personal importance of the trek made it a fitting goal for

Kyle. His extended timeframe made the goal more realistic, and an honest assessment of his physical capability, along with discipline, made it achievable. He ultimately bear-crawled up the entire mountain to the summit, a remarkable success.

A final note: effective goal setting facilitates learning and development. If your strategy includes a daily progress check-in, then there's a higher likelihood you'll remain focused and persistent. A daily review process allows for modification. Consider the way pilots monitor their flight course with small, consistent corrections in response to weather and turbulence to ensure safety and optimal flight time. If neglected, a plane's unchecked course could add hundreds of miles due to a shift in weather patterns alone. Approach your goals the same way. Several small corrections toward a known destination are more efficient than big swing backs.

A goal without a credible plan is just a wish. Too many people have poorly defined goals, and no real plan beyond a hope and a prayer. Having no plan means you *plan* to fail. It's invaluable to construct a bulletproof strategy for executing your SMARTP-FITS goals — and then fail forward fast!

F3 AND OODA LOOP

Once you jump out the door on a mission, the planning stages are over, and you are into the fail-forward-fast stage. In this stage of the success cycle, you will use the OODA Loop tool developed by late Air Force Lieutenant Colonel John Boyd. He was a fighter pilot with a brain for aircraft design and warfare conceptualization. He defined the instinctual expertise required to win rapid-fire, life-and-death aerial combat as the OODA Loop—a four-step process to fail forward to victory faster than your opponent by evaluating your relational position to the enemy (or competition) and making micro decisions to stay one step ahead of them. Though designed for fast maneuver warfare, it works extremely well for goal achieving, too. This is how it works:

Observe the situation closely to stay abreast of your relative position to the target. How is your progress affected by the competition, by the environment, by you and your team's attitudes, fatigue, biases, etc.? What are the strengths, weaknesses, and trends that could impact your success?

Orient and be ready to re-orient to the reality of what you observe. Those who observed and studied COVID-19 early were able to better assess and orient to the potential impact on their lives and businesses and pivot to thrive while others got hammered. What is your best next move? Where are the trends pointing? Are they just a fad or enduring? What is the gap that demands to be filled?

Decide what your next best course of action is. You may have to go back to FITS for this one, or you can use your best intuitive judgment if you need to move really fast. In other words, depending on the complexity and stakes involved, this step can be a simple choice, or a more complex decision made only after analyzing multiple options and courses of action.

Act. Doubt is removed through action. When you take action, that's how you obtain feedback, which you will observe and re-orient to again. Orient and then make another decision, and then act, and the cycle continues. The loop has no end to it. That is why it is a loop and not a linear process.

OODA LOOP

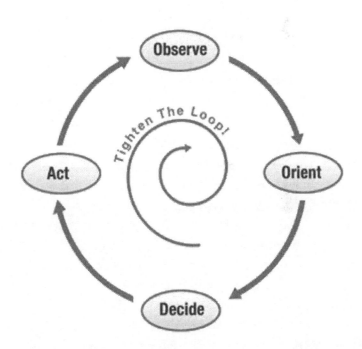

Your goal is to master the loop so you can minimize the time spent on each step until it is an intuitive and spontaneous process. In a highly competitive situation, a good strategy is to confuse or surprise your opponent into slowing down their OODA Loop processing time. This tool leads to easy, on-the-fly adjustments to your planning and decision-making. Use it to avoid getting stuck in groupthink, the planning-perfectionism trap, and leader bias.

This is what your plan would look like in action, when implementing the mental models:

- Create a KISS plan using SMARTP-FITS →
- Fail forward fast (F3) with rapid execution →
- Actuate the feedback OODA Loop →
- Develop new KISS plan →
- Execute again →
- Receive feedback and the success cycle continues →

VISUALIZE SUCCESS

You learned in the previous chapter how your mind can trick you. In this chapter, you studied a few mental models as an insurance policy against this. The final skill of mentally tough leaders is to change the content and energy of your mind through structured visualization.

Visualization is a powerful technique that will enhance your mental strength and allow you to tap into more of your mind power to accomplish more challenging tasks. It is the more advanced component of the law of "win first in your mind." As we discussed, many great inventors, entrepreneurs, and athletes use some form of visualization to create their desired outcomes in their minds first. It is time we made this a routine skill.

Visualization is the creation or recreation of an external experience in your mind. Early pioneers of this skill include my own swim coach at Colgate University. Coach Benson had me swim the two-hundred-meter breaststroke in my mind with a stopwatch before bed at night. Other sports psychologists and top coaches began using visualization to enhance performance in the '90s, and most Olympians report using it with great benefit in their training. There are two major forms of the practice of visualization.

Mental projection is visualizing a personal future state or victory. This is where you visualize images that create energy around a desired future experience before it happens "for real." I call this a "future me" visualization. You are envisioning an "ideal" version of yourself. Earning the SEAL Trident is an example of a future me visualization. Achieving a major milestone with a new business venture is another example. In either case, you create the event in your mind well before it happens. The visualized event is then charged with emotions, colors, sounds, scents, and tastes. You will reinforce those visual images through repeated practice sessions. This process plants a powerful seed in your subconscious mind. Then, as you work on achieving the goal (set according to SMARTP-FITS), your subconscious mind goes about supporting you with the resources necessary to nurture the event to its fruition. In a sense, you could say that visualization rewires your instinctual and emotional System 1 brain to keep it aligned with your goals—it's part of training the zookeeper.

The second form of visualization is *mental rehearsal*. A SEAL platoon will "dirt dive" a mission to set the patterns for winning in the mind prior to executing it for real. The SEAL operator will walk through a dive profile on dry land while visualizing every detail. In this manner, he performs all the major elements of the dive before ever getting wet. This was an important part of my mission prep when I was at SEAL Delivery Vehicle Team 1. The mini-sub dives were often six to ten hours in duration replete with complicated navigation patterns. Dirt diving the missions prior to launch proved crucial during the mission when fatigue and Murphy's Law reared their heads. The mental rehearsal implanted the route in the conscious and subconscious mind and provided a memory aid as well as subtle physiological cues. Additionally, mental rehearsal helped identify potential challenges before the mission hit the reality of the deep face-to-face.

Both forms of visualization can be performed from the first- or third-person perspective. They can be imaged from your objective frame, as if you were watching yourself in a movie, which would be from the third-person perspective. Or, you can visualize the event from your subjective frame, as if you were sporting a helmet camera and riding the rough terrain of your vision from the first-person perspective. Either method is effective, but most people start with the objective frame — watching themselves in the movie from the cheap seats — before migrating to the subjective frame as they gain experience.

Let's review why you will want to add this powerful tool to your mental tool kit. First, it leads to improved concentration in that the practice of visualization requires you to develop greater powers of concentration, due to the effort required to construct and maintain the visual imagery. In the early stages, the training can be frustrating, especially if you have difficulty holding an image in your mind for long. You may be more kinesthetic or auditory in nature (and developing the capacity to visualize will take patience).

Second, you will experience enhanced confidence as the result of the training. When you can clearly visualize an event in advance, your mental practice is accepted as real by your body. Though not as visceral as the physical doing of the event, the visual practice is still felt internally and empowers you. Research has proven that visualizing yourself throwing a basketball into a hoop leads to faster and better performance gains than just doing it for real. This is because you can practice the shots, sinking them perfectly in your mind every time, a feat difficult to pull off in the physical realm.

Additionally, if you fear performing to some degree, which we all do (especially for unsettling things such as public speaking), visualizing the performance repeatedly will dampen that fear response when you get to the live event and lead to more emotional control.

A final note on visualization: When done well, a visualized event involves the sensations of feelings, emotions, and sounds to support the imagery. The objective is to create as realistic a mental representation as possible, as if you are really experiencing it. That is what makes accomplishing th goal or task really possible....

Exercise 8: Create a SMARTP-FITS Goal

Start with Box Breathing for five to ten minutes.

Then — take out your journal and write down a goal using the SMARTP-FITS mental model. Choose something basic, such as my twenty double unders, or go bananas and envision yourself as the next president. Up to you! But make sure this goal FITS where you are now in life.

After you do that, take five minutes to visualize yourself attaining this goal. If this is your first time trying insight meditation, use the objective frame and watch yourself in the inspirational movie that ends with achieving your goal.

Now, go catch that goal!

• • •

Now that we understand the intricacies of our minds and have new skills for mentally tough leadership and kick-ass performance, let's turn our attention to becoming sheepdog strong and then to understanding and developing the five plateaus that every hero must traverse on their journey to self-mastery. The reality is, a true elite leader hones their skills and significantly advances personal evolution in the crucible of the team, becoming a master through the experience of helping others to master themselves. In other words, the synergy of a strong team elevates everyone's game. Let's look at how this is possible. Congratulations, you've made it through Section 2, and you're onto the third and final section of Book 1 of my *Unbeatable Mind* series.

You got this!

THE INTEGRATED SELF
IN ACTION

CHAPTER NINE

SHEEPDOG STRONG

"Let's not look back in anger, nor forward in fear, but around in awareness."

—James Thurber

The last of the SEAL ethos statements is "Earn your Trident every day." Earning your Trident every day is a reminder that the destination is never the goal. Once you become a SEAL, it is then incumbent upon you to seek and sustain the skills of the warrior and leader. The training is endless and relentless. You are never "there" and can never rest on the glow of past accomplishments. This is another powerful guiding principle for your life. The world changes so fast now you can't afford to throttle back or take things for granted. If you do, you will soon find yourself scrambling from behind, or watching from the sidelines, wondering what the hell hit you. Many companies and individuals in the past decade have made this mistake and faced irrelevance, an enterprise vanishing, or career gone bust because of it. Many believe that close to half of today's fortune 500 companies will be gone in five years due to technological disruption. Change or be marginalized is the new normal.

I learned in the SEALs how to embrace change while avoiding threats and remaining alert for opportunities using an offensive mindset. I call this being "Sheepdog Strong." Today's world can seem dangerous and chaotic. Becoming Sheepdog Strong will allow you to protect yourself and your loved ones in the event of a crisis, and it is essential to your ability to embrace change and earn your Trident of respect every day.

THE SHEEP AND THE WOLVES

Dr. David Grossman, author of *On Combat: The Psychology and Physiology of Deadly Conflict in War and Peace*, is a former Army officer who has studied the psychology of the warrior in combat. He metaphorically describes the vast majority of the world's population as sheep grazing in ignorant bliss of any threat, oblivious to any situational condition of what surrounds them. A much smaller percentage of the population, though, is comprised of wolves that make it their business to prey upon the sheep. The wolves are prone to violence and are comfortable taking what is not theirs, without conscience intervention. The wolves tear into the weaker sheep while the others, and society at large, pay scant attention. Fortunately, there are folks like you and me: A fractional percentage of the population who straddle the line between the sheep and wolves. This is the group Grossman passionately studies. He identifies us as sheepdogs. We keep our eyes on the wolves to protect the sheep. The sheepdog is the soldier, sailor, marine, coast guardswoman, police officer, ethical leader and Good Samaritan. It also needs to be you, if you are not there already.

During quiet times the sheep want little to do with the sheepdogs, feeling they are best if out of sight, out of mind. Sheepdogs can make people nervous because they sense that the sheepdog is comfortable with violence. My neighbor, when he didn't see me for a few days, assumed that I'd been gallivanting through foreign lands rolling up the bad guys. He loves that a SEAL is his neighbor, but I can tell that my knowledge, skill, and confidence make him nervous. Perhaps he fears that in mid-conversation I will lose it and rip his head off. Sheepdogs carry a heavy burden: though trained for violence, they are often the most disciplined and well-adjusted members of society. The sheepdog knows his Three Ps and One Thing and is committed to making a difference in the world through service. His violence differs greatly from the violence of the wolf — it is only used in defense and if absolutely necessary. Bound by a strict code of ethics and sense of duty, the sheepdog is trained to control the application of violence like a faucet meters water.

Recently I read the following headline: "Lost in Smartphones, San Francisco Train Passengers Didn't Notice the Gunman until He Pulled the Trigger." Scary, right? The smartphone is just the latest in a long line of external stimuli that have allowed many to act like sheep by taking the eyes off the important things in an endless distraction of info- and entertainment. TV started the trend, web surfing and social media saturated us with it, and now texting, tweeting and playing games on smartphones is putting the final nail in the coffin of awareness. The sheepdog has noticed this trend and learns to control use of the smartphone when his awareness is needed in public.

HERE ARE SOME RULES OF ENGAGEMENT:

1) Stop being passive. Commit to being a Sheepdog and making a difference. Pull your head out of the sand and pay attention to what is going on around you. Remember, you are earning your Trident of respect every day.

2) Activate your internal radar. We all have internal radars that can sense danger, but most people have them switched off. Marine Colonel Jeff Cooper's color system is helpful to learn here:

   a) Complete ignorance is white. Your internal radar is off; you are in the flock of sheep.

   b) Passive alertness is yellow. This is where your internal radar is switched on and passively scanning for threats.

   c) Super-heightened awareness is orange. This is when your radar pings a threat and goes on high alert, searching for information as to the threat level, potential action plans, resources, escape routes, weapons, etc. You are escalating your energy systems, getting ready for a fight.

   d) Action to counter is red. Your radar is redlining. This is when you tackle the jerk waving the gun before he pulls the trigger.

3) Initiate Sheepdog tactics. As a Sheepdog you can keep your smartphone to conduct business and text for help. However, learn to use it in a sheepdog manner. Here are the guidelines:

a) Always operate in yellow when in public.

b) Never be on the smartphone while walking, driving (duh), or in conversation with another human being.

c) When on public transit, scan the environment and sit near the back with a good view of the entire scene. Keep your smartphone off until you are certain there is no threat. Each time the bus/train/whatever comes to a stop, you turn it off and repeat the process.

d) In a restaurant or other open public space, enter by scanning the surrounding area outside and inside for any potential threats. If you detect a potential threat, then tune your radar to actively—but discreetly—scan in that direction. Sit with a good view of the establishment and enjoy your meal or experience and only check your smartphone in the bathroom.

e) Don't become paranoid. My purpose is to prod you to step it up and be part of the solution, but I am not recruiting a vigilante force. Forging an Unbeatable Mind and walking the warrior path means you are becoming uncommon, and the recommendations I offer are for you to put that uncommon excellence to good use. As we work on becoming better people every day, let's also step up to become Sheepdogs. That way we can protect the less aware, weaker elements of our wonderful society from the wolves. But don't mistake these recommendations for encouragement to go out looking for trouble, or to make some of your own.

OFFENSIVE MINDSET

The sheepdog will develop a mental "binary switch" that turns controlled violence on and off at will. It's important to know at a visceral, almost unconscious level that you are capable of shifting into a primordial survival mode instantly if you need to.

The "bamboo party" of my martial arts training is a good example of how I trained this binary switch. Four black belts place large bamboo poles over the ankles, hips, chest, and finally the throat of the brown belt candidate. Within seconds the flow of blood in your body is restricted such that instinctual fight-or-flight alarm bells go off. In that moment, you have to make a choice, and though it's a simulation, as far as your body and mind are concerned your choice in that split second is the difference between life and death. A nanosecond later, the student breaks free, shattering the bamboo poles and sending the black belts rolling in an explosion of energy and will that is practically reflexive. This experience gives you a powerful benchmark that anchors in the "knowing" that you can switch from orange to red in a heartbeat if you are ever pushed to the wall in a true "Sheepdog" situation. The "offensive mind training" I received taught me to control this binary switch, and also to throttle back down as the threat recedes.

My Ninjitsu Sensei, Shane Phelps, used to tell me that I had to always be the "subject" and never the "object" of the situations I enter in life, especially violent encounters. This means that we control the frame of the experience, create the lens that the other person looks through, and then write the script of what is unfolding before our very eyes. In this way we control the outcome and remain the victors. Consider my story about walking alone in Malaysia in Chapter Six, when I was confronted with several men who probably wanted to mug me. Instead, because I was Sheepdog Strong (and showed them my strength in mind, body, and spirit), they thought better of it and moved on, probably to some other poor unsuspecting guy who lacked the training and awareness that I had.

So, what if you don't classify yourself as a Sheepdog now but want to step up to be Sheepdog Strong? To start you will need to elevate your awareness to the "yellow zone" of passive alertness at all times in public. Begin to train yourself to see the threats before they escalate. I offered some practical rules of engagement earlier. Now, let's step it up.

DOG TRAINING

Sheepdog-strong training starts with training your awareness, but it quickly moves from that "I-Self" sphere of personal mastery to the "We-Team" sphere of team mastery. No sheepdog operates alone, you see; a team is required to tip the balance against the violent elements. Contrary to our cultural story of staunch, Dirty Harry-style individualism, it is teams of like-minded individuals who change the world. The following set of recommendations is offered to help you grow your sheepdog-strong team and eradicate fear.

Tip #1: Build a Sheepdog family. In a crisis situation, if you're spending all of your energy taking care of your family, which is common, you're not going to have as much energy to possibly help out your neighbors or community and be a part of the broader solution. If everyone's got some mental toughness skills and awareness development, they're more likely to be self-sufficient and can help you out, and that will allow you to turn your attention to other things. So have the color system discussion, and practice awareness drills, such as the Keep in Memory game (the KIM game is described in detail in the Unbeatable Mind Academy and is a way that SEALs use to train their memories and enhance awareness), travel mind games, and sensory awareness drills. Have fun with it but ensure that they understand the importance of training the tribe. If you don't have an immediate family, then this extends to your closest friends.

Tip #2: Build a Sheepdog network. When a hurricane devastated San Jose Del Cabo in Mexico this year, my brother-in-law, who has a home there, was visiting my family in San Diego. Luckily, he'd brought his daughter with him. However, this meant their home was left unprotected, and in the wake of the storm people were looting many neighborhoods in the area. My brother-in-law called up his daughter's boyfriend, whom he trusted and knew to be a Sheepdog, and asked him if he would check on their house. The boyfriend got a few of his buddies, fellow Sheepdogs, and they staged themselves in the house with their weapons for a few days until things calmed down. Looters ransacked much of the neighborhood, but not my brother-in-law's house. Natural disasters and even smaller local incidents can cause a crisis without warning, and you need to know how to take care of yourself and your loved ones. You can do that much more effectively if you're plugged in to a network of people who will all look out for one another.

Tip #3: Become a Sheepdog communicator. If you observe a situation or person who is obviously a potential threat, such as a suspicious man scoping the neighborhood several days in a row, take note and communicate it to your family and other Sheepdogs in your network. Don't be overly paranoid but err on the side of caution. Report things to the authorities that your network believes to be a clear and present danger. Don't expect them to do anything right away, though; just keep watching, and be prepared to act if necessary.

Tip #4: Prepare more than others. For instance, when you travel, take the following actions:

1. Review the travel route on a map and commit it to memory.
2. Print it out just in case. Phone GPS features are great until your battery dies or the signal disappears.
3. Locate some gas and food stops along the route and commit them to memory.
4. Fill your gas tank.
5. Check tire pressure on all five tires. (Don't forget the spare.)
6. Have a "just in case" bag ready with snacks, tools, LED flashlight, rags, and medical kit.

Tip #5: Be an undesirable target! This is a no-brainer but will require you to situate yourself and act differently in public. This can include carrying yourself more confidently and avoiding areas that make you vulnerable, that are not well lit, are desolate (such as large parking structures), or just give you the heebie-jeebies. Keep a high-power LED flashlight in your car. The flashlight should be able to blast about 1,000 lumens. If someone you don't recognize approaches you at night, blind them with the light and, if necessary, use it as a weapon. The light will ward off 99 percent of the wolves and give you time to escape as their night vision will be shot for a good five minutes.

Tip #6: Mentally prepare to do things you previously imagined unthinkable. This is tough for some people, and you don't have to go bonkers with it. Simply visualize yourself dominating a fight by kicking the groin, gouging eyes, and thumping the evildoer in the neck with your pipe arm. If you want self-defense training, I recommend Target Focus Training, Krav Maga, or attending our SEALFIT SOF Immersion Academy. When you can see yourself winning the fight in your mind, then you will be more likely to respond offensively and not freeze in a real-life situation.

A very real but extreme example is provided from one of my South African friends. There, car hijackers would stop people in their cars, simply shoot them, and then take off with their cars. In that environment you would not wait for the thug to come to your car but would use your car as a weapon and get out of dodge. Once I was in Kenya on a mission traveling on a highway when we passed a bus lying on its side. A fire was burning, and there appeared to be injured passengers inside. Our first instinct was to stop and help, but the Kenyan Special Forces driver skirted around it. He later told us it was a "honey trap" where the perpetrators were trying to bait sympathetic foreigners to stop so they could mug them, or worse, kidnap them for ransom. If our driver hadn't been mentally prepared for these kinds of threats, which are unique to his environment, who knows what fate may have befallen us? The world is dangerous and chaotic...destiny sure favors the prepared in body and mind!

A final note: being Sheepdog Strong requires that you set aside worry about what others think of you. Many may think your training and preparation to be extreme. Don't make a big deal of it because those same people will be running toward you, frantically waving their arms when something goes awry. At the same time, be very discreet and have fun with the training. It is not my intention to turn you into an outlier. Quite the opposite: I want you to be a leader and to be viewed as the one willing to go the distance to train and prepare body, mind, spirit, and team for some serious kick-ass if the wolves come around. This is admirable and, frankly, necessary if we are going to maintain order in a world going slightly mad. In the next chapter, we will further discuss how we can advance our performance with five critical skills for leaders to learn.

Exercise 9: The Body Scan
At the start of each Box Breathing practice session, I find a preparatory drill called the Body Scan to be useful. This drill helps align and relax the body and connect to the witnessing mind. The Body Scan doubles as a sensitivity

awareness exercise that can also be done as a stand-alone tool for intuition development. This — body awareness — is a great skill to have as we embark on our journey of becoming sheepdog strong. It brings attention to each part of your body, one at a time, and then to the experience of the whole. Awareness starts with ourselves and then branches out to others, just like the I, We, and It spheres.

For today's purposes, we're going to use the body scan as a relaxation technique before getting into five to ten minutes of Box Breathing.

As you move up your body, you will linger for a breath or two at each of the six subtle energy centers that run along the inside of the spine. These are known as chakras in the Yoga developmental system. This is what I touched on earlier when I brought up our energy body and the importance of breathing properly.

Here are your seven chakras, in order:

1. Root: located at the base of your spine. Color is red. Emotional energy is around survival, vitality, and feeling grounded.

2. Sacral: located about three inches above the root in your lower abdomen, below the navel. Color is orange. Emotional energy is around desire, healthy sexuality, and creativity.

3. Solar Plexus: located just below the ribcage. Color is yellow. Emotional energy is feeling powerful, joyous, and taking action.

4. Heart: located behind the heart in the center of the chest. Color is green. Emotional energy is love and connection.

5. Throat: located in the throat behind the Adam's apple. Color is blue. Emotional energy is clarity, attentiveness, and having a voice.
6. Brow or Third Eye: in the center of your brow but a couple inches behind. Color is Indigo. Emotional energy is wisdom, insight and, spiritual knowingness.
7. Crown: located at the top of the skull or slightly above. Color is violet. Spiritual energy is truth and integration.

To begin: Mentally scan your body from the feet to the top of the head. Pay attention to any sensations you may feel. Pause at each chakra to visualize the color and feel into the positive emotional energy it represents.

Once you complete the drill, expand your awareness to your entire being and get a sense for your unified body-mind-spirit.

Then expand that out a few feet in all directions to feel an interaction with the space around you. Try to sense the energy around you and inside you and try to feel connected to it all. If your mind wanders during this phase, don't sweat it...just bring it back to feeling the body and the space around you.

This exercise may seem esoteric if these practices are new to you but, trust me, it will have a profound impact over time. Feel free to write in your journal about any sensations that arose.

Now try Box Breathing for five to ten minutes. Don't forget to use a mantra if that helps you feel connected to the exercise.

• • •

Now let's turn our attention to other attributes we must sharpen, as a Samurai would a sword, to have of an offensive mindset. (Hey, maybe you *are* a Samurai!) In the next chapter, we will examine the Five Plateaus of the Unbeatable leader to provide a map to traverse, so you can evolve and track your developmental progress.

CHAPTER TEN

THE INTEGRATED SELF

"The deepest secret is that life is not a process of discovery, but a process of creation. You are not discovering yourself but creating yourself anew. Seek, therefore, not to find out who you are, seek to determine what you want to be."

—Neal Donald Walsch

William Wallace leading his clansmen in the movie *Braveheart*; King Leonidas leading his Spartans into battle in the movie *300*; *King Arthur*; *Spartacus*; *The Last Samurai*; and now the modern-day SEAL Marcus Luttrell of *Lone Survivor*—these are examples of the warrior-leader archetype in our media culture, some real and other fictional. The warrior hero is a source of inspiration, their character is different, and they seem to draw power from a mystical place. Portrayed in the films as larger than life, they serve as examples of the traits of mastery I want to discuss now. These traits include being unfazed in the face of imminent danger, being unquestionably sure about the action to take, and embracing the suck with silent fortitude. You may even know a real-life master yourself like I do.

Earlier I spoke about my first mentor, Kaicho Tadashi Nakamura, who displays the traits of mastery introduced in this chapter. He exemplifies a stoic strength, a beginner's mind and an uncommonly disciplined approach to his life. His character and example continue to inspire and influence me to this day, even though I am not training with him any longer. Many others, in all walks of life, are similarly humble and quiet professionals who strive to live up to the standards that masters like Kaicho Nakamura represent. Even though mastery seems like a goal or destination — and to a certain extent, it is — true masters know that a warrior will never stop learning, never stop pushing boundaries, and never stop growing. So masters focus on mastering the details of the journey every day, rather than the end-state. As stated above, the traits in this chapter are signposts on your journey and it is important to note that there is no perfection in any of them. There is only perfect trying, and the results will be informed by the stage of the journey and the personality of the student.

But sooner or later, the warrior will be called to step into the breach and serve beyond the call of duty. My friend, Glen Doherty, found himself in a situation, which tested his character in a way that warriors prepare for, but hope doesn't come. On September 11, 2012 the U.S. embassy outpost in Benghazi, Libya, came under a well-coordinated attack by terrorists. Glen, with an order to stand down, ignored the directive and raced to rescue the Americans under siege. He did not hang out and wait to hear about the tragedy later, or to be told what to do, but disobeyed orders to courageously act for the safety of others and putting his life at grave risk. Glen exhibited all the traits of mastery: single-point focus, uncommon resolve, a positively charged attitude, discernment, unflappability, fortitude, a focus on the welfare of others, and a humble acceptance of his responsibility. Glen's actions were directly responsible for saving eighteen American lives — but it led to his own demise. As you embark upon your own Unbeatable Mind journey, let the sacrifices of Glen and the traits of mastery he exemplified serve as an inspiration to stay the course and to never quit!

In this chapter, we'll take a look at the five developmental plateaus that every hero must traverse on their way to mastery in selfless service. We begin in *Survivor* mode, as a young entrant to the world. As security and confidence build, the hero expands out into *Protector* mode (or plateau). They will protect their family story and pet beliefs as they strive to achieve and be noticed. This third phase, *Achiever* mode, is an outward search for significance and meaning. It's vital to the journey but trapped in fixed thinking. Then, something sparks an interest in protecting the global commons (fighting for social equality and justice), so the hero joins a cause, moving up to their *Equalizer* plateau, fighting for their version of truth. But they do so at the expense of others. In the last phase of the hero's journey, they find mentorship from the master and, finally, understand they've been looking in the wrong places. They've been searching for themselves "out there." The master points out that the real answer lies within, where truth, wisdom, and love can be found. The hero ascends to the *Integrator* plateau, clearing up shadow and biases while holding onto values and lessons learned. They become world-centric in focus and action, deeply spiritual as opposed to religious, inclusive yet respectful of differences. They find peace, contentment, and universal love. A few even find enlightenment.

My first hero and mentor, Grandmaster Tadashi Nakamura, showed me what that fifth plateau looks like. He was different from anyone I had met up to that point. He exemplified a quiet, stoic strength with a beginner's mind and an uncommonly disciplined approach to life. His character and example inspire and influence me to this day. He never stops learning, never stops pushing boundaries, and never stops growing. He focuses on the details of his teaching and training every day, rather than worrying about how successful he is or the stress of running a worldwide organization. He is on a journey of self-mastery in selfless service from the fifth plateau of the Integrator.

THE FIVE PLATEAUS

The five plateaus are stages of development that serve as a map to appreciate the growth that has already occurred for you, and to point the way toward further vertical development. It's used as a self-diagnostic aide, a practice tool, and a psychoactive agent to stimulate deeper awareness of mental, emotional, and spiritual growth. Though I came up with the plateau names and descriptions, they closely correlate to the documented stages explored by experts in developmental and transpersonal psychology as well as Integral theory and Spiral Dynamics.

Though all the stages can be experienced at different moments throughout life's journey, we tend to settle in — or plateau — at one, depending on a plethora of circumstances: epigenetics, family of origin, cultural stage of development, life experiences, growth triggers, karma, etc. For our purposes, our aspiration is to ascend to the fifth plateau and continue our journey from there. Inclusiveness, world-centric concern and compassion, and perspective awareness are key skills that the Unbeatable leader will acquire at the fifth plateau.

I first published the matrix below in my teaming book, *Staring Down the Wolf*. I offer it here to give a snapshot of the map. You may find it helpful to take a picture and print it out. There's also a PDF at www.markdivine.com/unbeatablebook.

Plateau	Dominant Mountain	Sphere of Interest	Motivations	Healthy Emotions	Shadow Aspects	Unique Skills	Roles Archetypes
1st Survivor	Physical	Ego Self	Survival Family, Team 1st I got mine Power	Pride Boldness Love	Shame Excessive Fear	Brainstorming Bold Action	Conqueror Survivor Con Artist Gangster Lone Wolf Vigilante
2nd Protector	Emotional	Ego – Ethno local Self/Team-Tribe	Fundamentalist Traditional Rule bound Position / Rank Security	Courage Love	Guilt Jealousy	Setting Agenda Keeping Ground rules	Warrior Protector Freedom fighter Terrorist Bureaucrat
3rd Achiever	Mental	Ego – Ethno regional Self-Country	Self Reliant Independence Materialism Success	Ambition Drive Creativity Love	Careless Reckless Greed	Getting things done Entrepreneurial	Leader / CEO Chieftain
4th Equalizer	Intuitive	Ethno-World Country-Humanity	Sensitive Egalitarian Affiliation Tolerance	Caring Connecting Giving Healing Love	Spiritual Egotism Racism Class Envy or Anger	Relationship building	Philanthropist Do-gooder Activist Social-Entrepreneur Monk
5th Integrator	Kokoro	World Centric Humanity-Earth Cosmos	Process Interdependence of complex systems Win-Win Compassion Abundance Generous Service	Whole Peace Presence Love	Hyper-focus on development Too inclusive (missing trees within the forest) A-perspectival narrow-mindedness ("everyone is right") Spiritual Egotism Relationship detachment Aware of 1st-4th Plateau shadow - but unable to integrate	Managing Complexity Multiple Perspective taking and making	Strategist Global Thought Leader Healer - Shaman

Less than 5 percent of humanity is at the fifth Integrator plateau; roughly 30 percent are at the fourth Equalizer plateau; 35 percent are at the third Achiever plateau; roughly 20 percent are at the second Protector plateau, and about 10 percent have remained at the first Survivor plateau.

If we were looking, we would find those in developing, totalitarian, or war-torn areas to be stuck at the first and second plateaus due to life circumstances. (These are broad generalizations because, of course, any one individual can escape the grip of their life circumstances and grow beyond if they are called to it and have the courage to act   .) Europe, Canada, Australia, and New Zealand will see more fourth plateau Equalizers, with America and emerging market countries sharing a large percentage of third plateau Achievers. One's culture of origin can have a big influence on the attitude and growth prospect of its citizens.

Individuals can get stuck at a lower plateau of development and be completely ignorant of it. They just don't care. It doesn't make them bad people (unless they inherently are). They simply don't have the knowledge, desire, time, opportunity, or energy to work toward vertical growth. This is a classic *fixed mindset*, a great term that author Carol Dweck coined. We know these people. They're just existing, hanging out and happy with their lot or sad, angry, passive-aggressive victims with no desire to change. Some suffer through life in low-grade panic mode — distracted, over-burdened, chemically depressed, or in outright survival mode.

181

You, conversely, are here reading this and committing to maximum vertical growth, so that makes you extremely fortunate. But here's an early warning (you'll thank me later!): When entering a *growth mindset*, it's still easy to get stuck in a developmental rut, thereby stunting your growth. Or you could get trapped in a spiritual bypass or by egotism because you're struck stupid by your own newfound brilliance. That's why it's so important to include the BOO shadow work. If we don't investigate and eradicate the BOO shadow aspects at each plateau, our egos can trick us again and again.

The Buddha said it is rare for someone to learn of the paths of awakening to enlightenment, even more unusual to actually be on a path, and outright uncommon to achieve awakened awareness. But I predict many of you will be in that rarest category once you commit to this work. The Tibetans and yogis claim that achieving the highest level of integration and enlightened awareness is every human's birthright and eventual destination. It can be accomplished in one lifetime with disciplined practice or in seven to ten years with aggressive, immersive training. In this way, the Five Plateaus are a map for your own evolution, and the Five Mountains provides the framework for your training plan. But don't mistake the map for the terrain. The terrain is the actual embodied experience you are enjoying on this amazing journey of life.

WAKE UP, GROW UP, AND CLEAN UP TO SHOW UP!

My mentor, Ken Wilber, says that after "waking up" to your witness and calling, you are empowered to activate further "growing up." He goes on to say that in order to "show up" as the radiant, whole, spiritually aligned individual that is your True Self and essential nature, you must also "clean up" your shadow baggage. I concur, and that work has, for me, been harder and more painful than all the fancy meditation, yoga, breathwork, and visualization I have done in my life. (The Five Plateaus also serves as a practice tool to help guide you through the emotional mountain of clean-up you must endure to get to the next level of development.)

This is my biggest note yet: Do not judge yourself harshly or consider yourself less than if you can't imagine being at the fifth plateau right now! This is a universal feeling, and you would already be one of the 5 percent at the top if you were free of self-judgment and didn't judge others. But you're likely kicking back around the second, third, or fourth plateaus. We "include and transcend," integrating aspects of the earlier plateaus until we no longer feel constrained by them.

You see from the matrix that each plateau aligns with one of the Five Mountains, has an ego orientation, driving motivations, healthy emotions to embrace, shadows to overcome, unique skills or attributes, and archetypal roles. These details help to ground our understanding about where we are on the map.

Next, you will find a detailed description of each plateau. Read these with both your leader and teammate lenses on, and also from the perspective of the different roles you hold in your life. We have a dominant plateau but pull from the others. For example, when I was a Reserve SEAL, I would bring the positive aspects of my second plateau Protector self out as a sheepdog and military officer when I was on duty, while maintaining fifth plateau Integrator awareness of other teammates and foreign forces that had engaged us. At home, after the drill or extended period of service, I led with third plateau Achiever for my entrepreneurial initiatives, while maintaining fifth plateau awareness. In both cases, I tapped into the positive energy of an earlier plateau though my perspective was not limited to that level.

FIRST PLATEAU: THE SURVIVOR

Anyone that's in survival mode, whether it's from being born in a war-torn or impoverished region of the world, having absentee parents, or suffering a temporary loss of some kind can get locked here. The survivor lives a very physically oriented life, not having the time or luxury to care for the other four mountains of development. Taking care of basic survival needs dominates one's field of awareness, and self-actualization is a luxury afforded others. Prison populations and gangs are all first plateau cultures. A young child is at the first plateau until the brain develops enough to express some second plateau perspectives, generally after seven years or so. But, if something happens such as serious abuse, neglect, abandonment, the individual can get locked here into adulthood.

The survivor lives from an egocentric, self-centered worldview. Life revolves around "me" and, perhaps, a very small "we" — a close-knit family, tribe, or gang. Shadow elements of the first plateau include shame, fear, anxiety, anger, and victimhood. An unhealthy expression of this stage would lead to poor physical and mental health, perhaps using the body for instant gratification. Think of the unfortunate case of a sex worker or a brutish gang member. Both use their body (in different ways) to fulfill their immediate physical needs and desires, but these actions are usually taken without care or regard for the long-term costs or harmful effects to self and others.

Of course, this plateau has its positive side. Healthy growth at this stage sees healthy emotional and psycho-sexual development, the pursuit of sports, fitness, and good nutrition, and emotional expression can include boldness, love for family, and a non-quitting spirit.

Pride in one's success or team and mission can lead to stepping up to take bold action and just getting it done. Anger can be skillfully channeled into determination or drive. Anxiety can be managed through deep breathing and other stress management tools.

Unresolved first plateau shadows can be nasty when triggered. For example, my family of origin vacillated between the third and first plateaus. They were achievers with a successful business, material success, community engagement, and church involvement. However, behind closed doors, there were weekly rhythmic drops to the first plateau, triggered by alcohol abuse, rage, cynicism, and disrespect.

We want to look at our first plateau with the aim of developing the positive aspects and eradicating any negative BOO. A focus on developing a baseline of lifelong physical fitness, nutrition, sleep, recovery, and overall balance is a first plateau need. As these physical needs are met, then, at the psychological level, you will become aware of fear looping, anger triggers, depression, and any victim mentality so that you can move on. If life suddenly seems meaningless or pointless, then one has likely experienced new trauma or triggered early development trauma and has jettisoned back to the first plateau. This situation may resonate with you or someone you know. It needs to be addressed immediately, such as with a suicidal PTS inflicted veteran. Individuals can spiral quickly into destructive behavior. As a leader, you will deploy your stress arousal control skills whenever triggered into first plateau reactionary behavior or thinking: pause, breathe, think about what is triggering you, and act with attention control from a higher plateau perspective. When dealing with another individual who is either fixed or triggered into first plateau behavior and thinking, you will do what you can to mentor and help them through it, and then get support.

SECOND PLATEAU: THE PROTECTOR

The Second Plateau is the perspective of the Protector, who will go to great lengths to embody this role. These positions are downloaded from their family and culture of origin, and likely will go unexamined and unchallenged. The plateau has many positive qualities and comprises a large percentage of the population who uphold the structures, culture, and ideals of a traditional past. They believe in the superior nature of these comfortable structures and will fight to protect them. Many police, military members, and bureaucrats are fixed at the second plateau, while others tap into the attitudes to serve. Shadow aspects of this plateau can be seen in the football fan initiating a fistfight at the slightest insult to his team, extreme nationalism, tribal competition and conflict, etc.

We saw how decisions in the first plateau are largely instinctual in nature. At the second plateau, they tend to be made from emotional or deeply rooted biased patterns. Ego development is still self-centered with strong ethnocentric behavior at the community, team, and country levels. Classic archetypes of this plateau include the warrior, sheepdog, freedom fighter, the bureaucrat, and even the extreme shadow archetype of the terrorist...after all "one person's freedom fighter is another's terrorist."

Development to the second plateau occurs in a healthy individual as they embark into adulthood. Growing up in a dogmatic family or culture creates a strong tendency to get fixed at this plateau, leading to emotional immaturity and rigid rules. These individuals may not trust others who don't share their worldview and use emotions as a tool to get what they want — as opposed to using physical force (first plateau) or a logical argument (third plateau).

To navigate this plateau as a leader, you would want to see what second plateau perspectives you continue to hold onto and examine whether they still serve you. When dealing with other second plateau individuals, it's advisable to show respect for their traditionalist views and the value they offer, and then seek a win-win solution from your plateau perspective.

THIRD PLATEAU: THE ACHIEVER

Entrepreneurs, business leaders, most white-collar professionals, and gig workers reside at the third plateau. They (we) are out to succeed, develop financial security and independence, and climb the corporate ladder, with degrees and certificates adorning the walls.

Third plateau awareness comes from a blend of ego-centric, ethno-centric, and world-centric perspectives. Achievement and "scientific evidence" over social causes or spiritual development reigns. This plateau operates primarily from the mental mountain, specifically emphasizing rational left-brain thinking.

Third plateau individuals are self-reliant and have a hefty dose of ambition, creativity, and management skills, and a large capacity to love their families and teams.

Shadow aspects for those fixed at the third plateau can include obsession with work, leading to burnout and relationship stress, a carelessness toward the environment, antagonism toward competitors, and greed in general.

Third plateau achievers get shit done—from conceiving a business plan to raising money to hiring, managing, leading, running a clinic or law office, teaching in front of hundreds, giving speeches, etc. This plateau built the corporate and scientific infrastructures of the Industrial and Information Ages. It's also responsible for all the advanced technology now being utilized by angry first and second plateau survivors and protectors that are…against humanity. Not good. Third plateau archetypes will include CEOs, corporate chieftains, scientists, and scholars.

As a leader, you should consider whether you're an unbalanced, driven executive. Are you over-committed? Have you lost sight of your *why*? Is your health, the connection to your family, or your spiritual well-being suffering? Do you feel jealous when you see the material success of others? Is your level of success never good enough? Do you reserve your respect for the famous or others who have mastered material success? The self-determination and power of this plateau is seductive, but when achievement is at the expense of one's own health, growth, and a deep connection with other humans, it creates problems. How do you embody the best of the third plateau without giving up the benefits that achievers love so much? If you're a business owner, consider becoming a B Corporation and aligning with high standards for social and environmental good. Consider supporting (or starting) a philanthropic organization aligned with your purpose. I launched the Courage Foundation a few years ago to support the veteran community suffering from PTSD. Creating a fifth plateau mission that benefits humanity while doing no harm to the Earth, and then executing it with your positive achiever mindset could have the biggest impact. It was third plateau individuals and thinking got us where we are now as a culture, bringing us into the modern industrialized world. And it will be the third plateau thinking and behavior — but from a fifth plateau level of development — that will evolve humanity toward a more balanced and positive future.

FOURTH PLATEAU: THE EQUALIZER

This brings us to the fourth plateau. The Equalizer is a sensitive individual who would like everyone to be treated the same. It is the Equalizer in government that calls for nationalized healthcare, sanctuary cities, and supports the Black Lives Matter movement. They are the social activist who denounces business excess and profit motives that create wealth inequality. Seeing themselves as the modern equivalent of Robin Hood, they want government to take from the rich and give to the poor. But the Equalizer can also be an elitist academic or journalist who aspires to be associated with a global community of do-gooders but has no problem taking full advantage of their country's assets while paying as little taxes as possible.

My comedian friend, JP Sears, hilariously pans the fourth plateau shadow elements of Equalizers with their proclivity toward spiritual-egotism, yoga retreats, micro-dosing and other body-brain hacks. The heart of the equalizer is in the right place, but it often doesn't have any room to include those that don't see things their way.

The pesky shadow of this plateau can come out in insidious ways, including reverse racism and class envy (as the Equalizer rails against the 1 percent as the source of all problems). Positive skills that fourth plateau individuals embody include relationship building, breaking down old, ineffective institutional boundaries, and generating awareness for important causes. Role archetypes include philanthropists, activists, social entrepreneurs, and monks.

Generally speaking, this plateau is free from the survival needs of first plateau, from the fixed conformism of second plateau, and from the fixation on material success of the third plateau. Most people reading this would fall into this group but may be slightly put-off by my depiction of the shadow side of the plateau. If that is you, please know that this map is neither a hierarchy nor a judgment of others. We all have the "lower plateaus" in us, with positive attitudes as well as shadow elements. The point is to use the map to identify growth opportunities, to clear up the shadows of each plateau, and to ascend to the integrated stages of conscious awareness. Most highly educated business and community leaders, media, arts, medical, academic, nonprofit, or "deep state" professionals are either fixed here or passing through this plateau, with strong mental, emotional, and intuitive energy directed toward a higher-order purpose and self-actualization.

FIFTH PLATEAU: THE INTEGRATOR

The Integrator has the perspective of a world-centric leader with whole mind, or kokoro, consciousness. The Integrator has transcended and included the first four plateaus, while working to eradicate shadow elements that trigger negative conditioning in each. Integrators have the capacity to engage the positive qualities of each plateau while leading, and to take the perspectives of teammates and organizational cultures locked into, or triggered by, the first four plateaus. In addition, the Integrator is mastering development and integration of the Five Mountains and aligned with their calling in a powerful mission. The ego has taken a back seat to the witness, allowing the Integrator to have genuine compassion for all of humanity and the Earth.

The integrator works on developing authentic and compassionate communication skills, which make them great negotiators and healers. They enjoy building and curating interdependent complex systems and seeking win-win relationships and outcomes that consider second, third, and fourth order consequences. Compassion, abundance, generosity, service — these are the virtues of the world-centric leader.

Negative thinking and emotions have largely been eradicated, though there may still be work to do (of which the Integrator is aware). The integrator is present and stands their ground with courage. They practice and seek non-attachment, acceptance, forgiveness, peacefulness, love, and abundance. The integrator is not immune to painful or negative emotions, but when these arise, they will allow the experience to run its course and surrender the energy to the Universe, so that it does not develop any new negative conditioning. They process in a way that doesn't deny, project, or repress the emotion.

There are some nuanced shadow aspects of the fifth plateau. There could be a hyper-focus on one's own personal development to the exclusion of other important things in life. Someone could be at the Integrator plateau but be grossly out of shape, which will trigger a first plateau crisis sooner or later. Finally, an integrator can "try too hard" and end up complicating their mission. They can miss the trees within the forest, as not every mundane issue needs a committee of compassionate elders to fix it. The other side of that coin is the possibility of the perspective that "everyone is perfect the way they are" and also "right from where they are." Though this may have some spiritual truth, it can lead to pacifism, allowing the wolf into the henhouse. Spiritual egotism of the fourth plateau could still rear its ugly head...as well as relationship detachment due to over-development of the higher chakras (head in the clouds) and under-development of the lower, grounding chakras (feet on the ground). Finally, the Integrator may be well aware of shadow in other plateaus but lack the skillful means or energy to deal with it effectively.

LEADING FROM THE FIFTH PLATEAU

Leadership from the fifth plateau means having the ability to manage your team skillfully and authentically, with all its multiple perspectives and complexities. The integrator will use their powers to help heal the planet, end the investment in sanctioned violence, and connect globally at a deeper level. Archetypes of this plateau include strategists, global thought leaders, and healers who have transcended the limits of tribe or national identity, but respect and enjoy the distinctions and boundaries of cultures. As you deepen your Unbeatable Mind training toward self-mastery, your perspectives, conscious awareness, attitude, and empathy will stabilize at the fifth plateau. It's worth noting that the fifth plateau is not the "final" stage of development, as consciousness has a primal drive to evolve, but it's a great goal for this lifetime.

Where you're at is your developmental "center of gravity" to date. You may find that, at your finest moments or on social media, you identify with the fifth plateau as the type of person seen advocating for the environment and global human rights and believes (cognitively) in the interconnectedness of all beings. But at work, you can't stand the judgmental jerks you're surrounded by, and the parents in your kid's class are total prima donnas. You hit the CrossFit workout three times a week and aren't 100 percent sure if you did 100 pullups...maybe it was only 85, and you pretended it was 100 to win the workout. Your side gig exists to save enough money so that you can retire and play golf in five years. See where this is going?

Those behaviors are not uncommon for a third plateau social climbing Achiever who wants to look like a fifth plateau global philanthropist. Fixed mindset individuals will demonstrate most, if not all, the attitudes of a single plateau, but succumb to the behaviors from earlier developmental stages. The more evolved and aware we become, the more fluidly we can navigate between the plateaus with awareness. As we stabilize at the fifth plateau, we'll spend less and less time in the lower plateaus because of our growing spiritual orientation of non-attachment to positionalities, judgments, and even desire.

The late Stephen M.R. Covey wisely said: "Seek first to understand and then to be understood." We can get very attached to our own beliefs and worldviews. It takes courage to navigate the plateaus to see one's truth clearly. If you operate primarily from a third plateau Achiever consciousness yet dip into a second plateau Protector and first plateau Survivor when triggered or stressed, the good news is you're now aware of it! You won't get stuck there! You can use the Unbeatable Mind tools and practices as an opportunity for further growth and propel back up. Yeah! We can use the plateau stage model of development as a tool to spur continuous vertical evolution.

• • •

We are almost finished with our journey together. Consider reading the book multiple times, as it reveals new secrets as your unbeatable mind opens up to seeing them. I hope you continue to study these effective tools and find it's true for you, as well. The journey of a thousand miles starts with a single step — and "breath" — and you have already begun. Now take another and turn it into a daily Box Breathing practice, maybe a morning ritual. Soon, you'll be well on your way to becoming unbeatable.

Exercise 10: Identify Your Plateau and Set a Goal

Start with the body scan to create awareness of self and the energy around you. Then, move on to five or ten minutes of Box Breathing.

Next, open your journal and answer these questions:

- What plateau do you most identify with now as your center of gravity?
- Where do you see yourself a year from now?

Wrap up with a contemplation meditation to launch your journey to the next plateau. See yourself in a story you want to manifest in your life. Or put the camera helmet on and envision the success of this event/goal/challenge from a first-person perspective.

And then don't forget to write about it in your journal afterward.

Now, we are radically focused and in alignment with our powerful vision, purpose, mission, and stand. We are also tapping into whole-mind thinking to master ourselves in service to humanity.

You are on your way to reaching your 20X potential to forging mental toughness and emotional resiliency. You are creating an unbeatable mind.

Awesome work!

AFTERWORD

A few months after graduating from BUD/S training, I reviewed a book written by my mentor, Kaicho Nakamura, *One Day, One Lifetime*, a collection of the Zen meditation lectures I had experienced the prior four years. The saying, "one day, one lifetime" has stayed with me since, and serves as a reminder that every day is important and could be my last. I have learned to live each moment fully and in the present and avoid treating even a single day as a dress rehearsal.

This same attitude is required of self-mastery, which will be achieved as you develop your personal Five Mountains and integrate at the Fifth Plateau. Ultimately, you will experience this integration as a union of your rational mind, your heart, and your witnessing self. With this integration, you will begin to experience more presence and will use your whole mind for creative and holistic thinking. Your actions will be powerful and positive. A presence will be enjoyed, whether sitting in silence or performing a workout or problem-solving through a critical project—or even if you find yourself in a fight for your life. The signposts that indicate you are making progress on this incredible journey include:

- Experiencing increasing moments of peace
- Sensing an expanding field of awareness
- Being able to perceive truth better—cutting through the nonsense of the world
- Feeling more love for your fellow humans and for all sentient beings

- Feeling a sense of urgency to become a steward for Earth
- Finding you can accomplish any worthy task you set your mind to
- Tapping into your intuition and gut feelings frequently and using this skill to make wise decisions
- Finding beauty and grace even in mundane or dismal situations
- Experiencing true selflessness

On April 23, 1910, Theodore Roosevelt delivered a speech whose words have inspired generations of warriors and leaders since:

> It is not the critic who counts; nor the man who points out how the strong man stumbles, or where the doer of deeds could have done them better. The credit belongs to the man who is actually in the arena, whose face is marred by dust, sweat and blood; who strives valiantly; who errs, who comes up short again and again, because there is no effort without error and shortcoming; but who does actually strive to do the deeds; who knows great enthusiasms, the great devotions; who spend himself in a worthy cause; who at the best knows in the end the triumph of high achievement, and who at the worst, if he fails, at least fails while daring greatly, so that his place shall never be with those cold and timid souls who neither know victory or defeat.

Mr. Roosevelt was articulating the value of avoiding the deathtrap of gossip and other mindless distractions and staking your life on a path of boldness; of translating this boldness into action, to never drift or shirk from defending your values, to stand your ground and never sway. He's talking about acknowledging and honoring your passion by taking aim with that passion and shooting for the moon. Only through bold action can we make physical contact with our working limitations, and then shatter them again and again.

The antithesis of boldness is to stall. Boldness shrivels up and dies when you say today is no good and that you'll start tomorrow. The energy is drained during hesitation's perpetual spin. Waiting for the perfect time to act—until you have the complete kit bag full of tools and weapons, or the perfect partner, or some perfect orchestration of conditions. This sort of delay will leave you back with those timid souls who know neither victory nor defeat.

But, as you have learned, taking bold action doesn't mean that we are always acting. Many mistake constant action for productivity and progress. The Warrior's Way is to first plan for bold action, win in the mind, bulletproof the mission and then, act with boldness. And during this state of action and execution there are moments to take pause and evaluate the battlefield to see what has changed since you acted last. In this pause you will reorient yourself, your team or organization to the new reality. You'll devise new tactics and a fresh strategy, and with this invigorated plan explode out of the blocks with boldness. In this process there is a balanced flow between acting, observing, thinking and acting again. Boldness requires this balance, or it can quickly look like foolishness.

So how can you develop your facility with boldness? Here are some ideas to ensure boldness in life and business:

- Hang around people who are doing bold things and study their way. I offered an Unbeatable Mind seminar once at an event for a non-profit called Operation Underground Railroad. Tired of seeing nothing being done to stop the insidious sex slavery trade, this group has decided to take massive bold action. In 2014 they rescued over 300 girls from slavery in South America. It's as if they listened to Roosevelt's speech and immediately banded together and went for it. This is the type of bold to model.
- Take action before you think you are ready. I do this all the time and then have to make course corrections, or refund customers when something breaks and rebuild it in flight. But I have no regrets about this approach. A good example is the Unbeatable Mind Academy, where I finished developing each lesson literally days before it was due to be delivered to the customers in 2012.
- Whatever you think you can do, think bigger. With three billion people due to come online via mobile devices in the next three years, I encourage you to think bigger with your business and professional goals than you think you can right now. Why not impact a million or even a billion people?

- Train to be bold. Commit to taking the information in this book and applying it into a custom integrated training regimen.

Unbeatable Mind training will embolden you and steer you away from becoming one of the critics, one of those who waste precious energy illuminating the faults and failures of others. I am asking you to get into the arena and taste the sweet joy of victory and capture the precious lessons of defeat. Training must be constant and relentless. Push yourself to find new 20X limits, test your grit daily and stay in the arena, never shying from a challenge. Set audacious goals and knock them down one incremental victory at a time. Push your development to the Fifth Plateau and you will soon stand out in all you do. You will be uncommon and live each day as if it were a lifetime. It's your time now, so step up and be Unbeatable!

TEN SECRETS TO SUCCESS

This book has covered a lot of ground and we've swam deeply into some areas you may never have thought about before. As you know by now, finishing the book doesn't mean you have finished your journey; in fact, it's just beginning! To help you stay on track, I will leave you with a list you can copy into our journal or tear out of the book to refer to at least once a day as a reminder of the path you've chosen. I hope that it inspires and reinvigorates you as much as it does me.

1. Live an examined life and embrace sacred silence.
2. Know your One Thing, your purpose, passion, and principles.
3. Connect all your small actions to these.
4. Develop mental and emotional control: master the Big Four of Mental Toughness and Emotional Resiliency.
5. Challenge yourself to find your 20X and improve daily.
6. Turn to others in service and develop a winning team.
7. Align to win in all three spheres of I, We, and It.
8. Select SMART-FITS targets.
9. Employ KISS "good-enough" planning.
10. Take massive action, and then fail forward fast. And never, ever quit.

Hooyah! See you in training!

Mark Divine

ABOUT THE AUTHOR

Mark Divine is a creative developer of cutting-edge training for warriors, athletes, leaders, and teams. His innovative programs include the mental toughness and functional fitness program **SEALFIT,** the whole person leader and team development program **Unbeatable Mind,** the integrated yoga system **Kokoro Yoga,** and the veteran healing nonprofit The **Courage Foundation.** His books include the NYT bestsellers *Staring Down the Wolf* and *8 Weeks to SEALFIT,* the Amazon and WSJ bestsellers *The Way of the SEAL, Unbeatable Mind,* 3rd Ed., *Kokoro Yoga,* and *Uncommon.*

Originally from Upstate New York, Mark holds an undergraduate degree in Economics from Colgate University and an MBA in Finance from New York University Stern School of Business. Mark's first career was with Coopers & Lybrand (now PriceWaterhouse Coopers) as a Certified

Public Accountant. Four years after joining Coopers, Mark left behind the corporate world to pursue his vision to become an elite Navy SEAL officer. At twenty-six, he graduated as Honor Man (#1-ranked trainee) of his SEAL training class number 170. Perhaps even more striking was that his entire original boat crew graduated with him that day. The odds of that happening by chance are literally one in a million. That was no accident. It was the first of many elite teams that Mark Divine built. Mark went on to serve for nine years on active duty and eleven as a Reserve SEAL, retiring at the rank of Commander in 2011.

Because he was so effective in developing the physical, mental, leadership, and team skills needed for success in battle, in 2005 Naval Special Warfare Group One hired Mark to run their pre-deployment certification training. For the same reason, in 2006 the Navy Recruiting Command hired him through his company SEALFIT to create and launch the national Navy SEAL Mentor program for new recruits. This hugely successful initiative helped increase the quality of SEAL candidates and reduced the BUD/S attrition rate by up to five percent.

Through his innovative SEALFIT and Unbeatable Mind training systems, including the Hell Week simulation Kokoro crucible, Mark provides the physical, mental, and emotional tools and coaching that allow not 15 percent but 90 percent of his trainees to lead and succeed in the most demanding training in the world…and in combat. He now shares the same secrets to entrepreneurs, executives, and teams through his books, speaking, award winning podcast, and world-renowned leadership.

What make Mark's programs so effective is his focus on the whole person — training the physical, mental, emotional, intuitive, and spiritual aspects together. In his time leading Special Operations Forces missions, he'd seen the power of a deep emotional heart connection. He experienced the gut's intuition to save himself and teammates on more than one occasion. He could see first-hand the importance of merging head, heart, and gut into our decisions and actions. Mark knew that these skills would be extremely important for future leaders, and that they could and should be trained.

Today, Mark centers his time around service and teaching to share his five-mountain philosophy with as many people as possible. Motivated by an authentic desire to serve others, Mark envisions a resilient and peaceful global leadership with a determined goal of influencing 100 million world-centric leaders by the year 2040. Every day, in every way, Mark seeks to inspire generations, old and young alike, to discover their true 20x potential in life. Hooyah!

To learn more about Mark Divine, his programs, or to engage in training, visit:

www.markdivine.com
www.unbeatablemind.com
www.SEALFIT.com
www.feedcourage.org

TRY THE UNBEATABLE MIND 20X SYSTEM FOR FREE!

Because you purchased this book, we are inviting you to try our Unbeatable Mind 20X System for free. This system gives you the ultimate way to unlock your massive 20X potential in every area of your life. You'll get:

- 30 days of virtual training and coaching with Mark Divine—on demand and on your schedule
- The same 20X system and tools that have been the foundation of our work with the Navy SEALs, Team USA Olympics, and elite Fortune 100 companies
- Step-by-step coaching on how to install the full system into your life in just 30 days
- Our proven 20X rapid planning tools to help you achieve your most important goals over the next 12 months—health, business, career, fitness, relationship, financial, and more
- Lasting Unbeatable Mind habits and routines that can help you achieve your 20X potential for the rest of your life

Register to try it for free today!
Go to: www.unbeatablemind.com/bookoffer

7 LEADERSHIP COMMITMENTS THAT FORGE ELITE TEAMS

NEW YORK TIMES BESTSELLER

MARK DIVINE

U.S. NAVY SEAL & FOUNDER OF SEALFIT

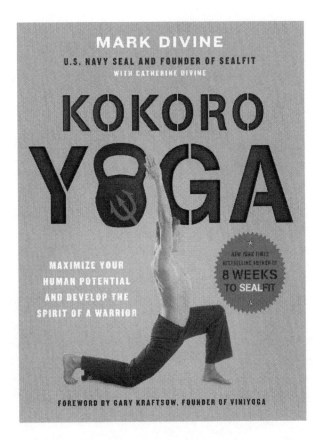

Kokoro Yoga, by *New York Times* bestselling author and former US Navy SEAL Mark Divine, is an integrated physical, mental, and spiritual training, designed initially for the nation's elite special-ops soldiers and now taught to anyone seeking to develop the heart and mind of a warrior. Kokoro, the Japanese concept of warrior spirit — or merging heart and mind into action — is the central focus of Divine's new approach to teaching yoga.

RESOURCES

As I review new books and reference them in our Unbeatable Mind Academy online program, I update the Unbeatable Mind Reading List online at:
www.unbeatablemind.com/readinglist
Check it out!

UNBEATABLE
MIND

Made in the USA
Columbia, SC
21 June 2022